T0365327

Cambridge Elements

Elements in Second Language Acquisition
edited by
Alessandro G. Benati
University College Dublin
John W. Schwieter
Wilfrid Laurier University, Ontario

PROCESSABILITY THEORY

Manfred Pienemann
Paderborn University
Anke Lenzing
University of Innsbruck

Shaftesbury Road, Cambridge CB2 8EA, United Kingdom

One Liberty Plaza, 20th Floor, New York, NY 10006, USA

477 Williamstown Road, Port Melbourne, VIC 3207, Australia

314–321, 3rd Floor, Plot 3, Splendor Forum, Jasola District Centre,
New Delhi – 110025, India

103 Penang Road, #05–06/07, Visioncrest Commercial, Singapore 238467

Cambridge University Press is part of Cambridge University Press & Assessment,
a department of the University of Cambridge.

We share the University's mission to contribute to society through the pursuit of
education, learning and research at the highest international levels of excellence.

www.cambridge.org
Information on this title: www.cambridge.org/9781009571920

DOI: 10.1017/9781009375931

First published 2025

A catalogue record for this publication is available from the British Library

ISBN 978-1-009-57192-0 Hardback
ISBN 978-1-009-37594-8 Paperback
ISSN 2517-7974 (online)
ISSN 2517-7966 (print)

Additional resources for this publication at www.cambridge.org/Pienemann

Processability Theory

Elements in Second Language Acquisition

DOI: 10.1017/9781009375931
First published online: March 2025

Manfred Pienemann
Paderborn University

Anke Lenzing
University of Innsbruck

Author for correspondence: Manfred Pienemann, pieneman@mail.upb.de

Abstract: Processability Theory (PT) is a psycholinguistic theory of second language acquisition. The theory builds on the fundamental assumption that learners can acquire only those linguistic forms and functions which they can process. Therefore, PT is based on the architecture of the human language processor. PT is implemented in a theory of grammar that is compatible with the basic design of the language processor. This Element gives a concise introduction to the psycholinguistic core of PT – showing that PT offers an explanation of language development and variation based on processing constraints that are specified for typologically different languages and that apply to first and second language acquisition, albeit in different ways. Processing constraints also delineate transfer from the first language and the effect of formal intervention. This Element also covers the main branches of research in the PT framework and provides an introduction to the methodology used in PT-based research.

Keywords: Processability Theory, second language acquisition, language processing, psycholinguistics, second language development and variation

ISBNs: 9781009571920 (HB), 9781009375948 (PB), 9781009375931 (OC)
ISSNs: 2517-7974 (online), 2517-7966 (print)

Contents

Preface 1

1 In a Nutshell: What Is Processability Theory About? 1

2 Key Concepts 2

3 Main Branches of Research 35

4 Implications for SLA Theory 70

5 Implications for Pedagogy 75

6 The Constructive Strategy of PT in Theory Building 84

7 Key Readings 85

References 87

Preface

Writing this Element on Processability Theory has been a team effort. Anke Lenzing and Manfred Pienemann are the authors of the main body of the text that is complemented by summaries of additional aspects, extensions and practical application of Processability Theory authored by the original researchers. These summaries are presented in six Info Boxes that are highlighted in blue and positioned in thematically related sections of this Element.

The topics of the Info Boxes and their authors are as follows:

(1) THE TYPOLOGICAL PLAUSIBILITY OF PROCESSABILITY THEORY FOR JAPANESE L2

Satomi Kawaguchi, University of Western Sydney, Australia

(2) STABILISATION: THE CASE OF BONGIOVANNI

Howard Nicholas, La Trobe University, Australia

(3) A QUICK SUMMARY OF GENERATIVE ENTRENCHMENT

Manfred Pienemann, University of Paderborn, Germany

(4) SYNTACTIC DEVELOPMENT IN RUSSIAN AS A SECOND LANGUAGE

Marco Magnani, Trento University, Italy

(5) DEVELOPMENTALLY MODERATED FOCUS ON FORM

Bruno Di Biase, University of Western Sydney, Australia

(6) TASKS HAVE A GREAT POTENTIAL FOR TARGETED LANGUAGE LEARNING IF THEY INCLUDE A FOCUS ON THE DEVELOPMENTAL READINESS OF L2 LEARNERS

Jana Roos, University of Potsdam, Germany

1 In a Nutshell: What Is Processability Theory About?

Like so many things in life, second language acquisition (SLA) is a somewhat mysterious thing because there is no obvious explanation for how the human mind makes it work. What we know by observation is that SLA flows like a river – following its own course. And like a river (to continue this metaphor), its flow is partly predictable and partly variable, sometimes chaotic and sometimes it dries up. Even after more than half a century of research on SLA there is no one theory that can explain the majority of the key mechanisms underlying SLA. Several theories focus on factors such as motivation or interaction, seeking to identify factors that 'cause' aspects of the flow of SLA. In contrast, Processability Theory (PT) focuses on an aspect that is INTERNAL to the flow. This internal aspect can be compared with the way the riverbed forces the water through channels defined by certain bounds. Formally, such bounds are known as constraints. PT focuses on the way the human mind constrains SLA. In the same way that water cannot just flow in any direction, the human mind is limited in the way it can process and store bits of the second language (L2).

PT makes the workings of these constraints of the human mind explicit in the same way as hydrology and geology make explicit the impact of the riverbed on the flow of water. 'Making explicit' means that a formal theory is used that can generate predictions about the flow of water/SLA. Not every aspect of the flow can be predicted, but several key aspects can, including the limits within which the flow can vary. All of this has important repercussions for the prediction of floods (in the case of rivers) and predictions of which bits of the L2 can be learnt at what point along the course of the L2 'river's' journey.

Being able to make such predictions means a lot, not only for the explanation of SLA, but also for knowing which aspects of the L2 are learnable at what point. Processing constraints do not explain all aspects of the SLA mystery, just like the riverbed does not explain all aspects of the flow of a river. But constraints are an essential and necessary component of an overall explanation.

In this Element we hope to set out in an accessible way what processing constraints are, how we can make them explicit, how they can account for the general flow of SLA, and how they can formally delineate its variability. PT applies to the human mind in general and the way its constraints operate across languages. Therefore, we will use examples from English SLA as well as from the SLA of very different languages such as Japanese.

Explaining things relating to the human mind is the business of philosophy. Therefore, we will also look at what constitutes an explanation, what kinds of explanations there are, and how different approaches to SLA view these matters – attempting to sort out where there are contradictions and where different approaches are complementary.

2 Key Concepts

2.1 Explanation by Cause and Explanation by Constraint

Many readers will associate the image of leaves rustling in the wind with an implicit cause-and-effect relationship.[1] The wind makes the leaves move. The wind is the cause. The movement of the leaves is the effect. It is not uncommon for SLA researchers to look for cause-and-effect relationships in an attempt to account for SLA phenomena. In Section 1, we mentioned motivation as one

---

[1] This section is based in part on the following conference presentations by Manfred Pienemann: 'PT and co: How constraints explain SLA'. PALA 2022, 21–23 September 2022, International Islamic University, Malaysia; and 'What sort of an animal is PT? And how does it relate to other species?' PALA 2023, 14–15 September 2023, University of Innsbruck, Austria.

possible causal factor. For instance, Dörnyei and colleagues (e.g. Dörnyei et al., 2015) studied the impact of motivation on SLA in great detail. Some researchers (e.g. de Bot et al., 2007; Larsen-Freeman, 2017) go as far as assuming that, ideally, one needs to consider ALL causal factors affecting SLA to be able to account for SLA. de Bot et al. (2007, p. 18) even believe that an approach to explaining SLA cannot be correct if it is based on only one factor, as in their view it is the interplay of all factors that causes SLA to take the shape that it does.

So is it futile to pursue an approach to SLA that focuses on processability – without including causal factors? To be able to answer this question we need to look in some more detail at the nature of explanations in SLA research and what it means for the construction of an overarching theory of SLA.

A scientific explanation is required when one encounters an observation that cannot be explained in a way that is not self-evident and that does not follow in an obvious way from another observation. For instance, in many empirical studies of the SLA of English, it has been found that learners of English as a second language (ESL) with different first language (L1) backgrounds initially produce a Subject-Verb-Object (SVO/SVX) pattern in Wh-questions (Pienemann, 1998a, pp. 177–181) – for example:

(1)   * When we go home?

In other words, beginning learners simplify Wh-questions such as the one given in (1) by leaving out the auxiliary that would be required in native English as in (2):

(2)   When will/do we go home?

The effect of the omission of the auxiliary is that the learner avoids placing the auxiliary in a position left of the grammatical subject (*we*), thus producing the same basic word order as in statements (i.e. *We go home*) and also avoiding the requirement for 'auxiliary inversion' in Wh-questions.[2]

PT explains the initial avoidance of auxiliary inversion in Wh-questions by beginning ESL learners as follows: beginning ESL learners initially follow an SVO pattern in Wh-questions *because* they are unable to process 'subject–auxiliary inversion'. The reader will have noticed straightaway that an important part of the PT-based explanation is missing from this simple because-statement, namely the exact reasoning why beginning ESL learners are unable to process subject–auxiliary inversion. We would be getting ahead of our story about PT if we were to outline the exact psycholinguistic and formal details of reasoning behind PT at this point.

---

[2] https://en.wikipedia.org/wiki/Subject%E2%80%93auxiliary_inversion.

Instead, we will offer a brief plain-English summary for now, and we will return to this point in more detail in Sections 2.2–2.4.

The basic hypothesis underlying PT is that the architecture of the (human) language processor constrains the range of linguistic forms that the learner is able to process at any given point in development. This hypothesis is illustrated in Figure 1 where the language processor is depicted as a maze-like structure in the learner's mind that 'filters' the linguistic forms of the L2. Obviously, this is nothing more than a simple graphic illustration, but we hope that it may be useful for readers unfamiliar with PT.

Returning to the issue of explanations, we would like to draw the reader's attention to the relationship between observation and explanation. An observation that is not self-evident such as the Wh-SVO question shown in example (1) and that does not follow in an obvious way from another observation such as the prominent SVO patterns in Wh-questions produced by beginning ESL learners is referred to

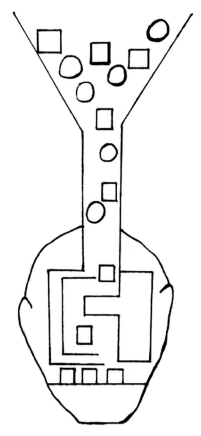

Figure 1 How the language processor constrains L2 acquisition
(© Anton Dörner).

as an *explanandum* (the thing that needs to be explained). The question underlying the explanandum is a why-question: why do ESL learners initially follow an SVO pattern in Wh-questions? The answer to this question – that implies a 'because' – is the *explanans* (the thing that explains the explanandum): 'because beginning ESL learners are unable to process subject–auxiliary inversion'.

Even without knowing further details about the internal logic of the PT explanation of initial word orders in ESL acquisition, it is clear at this point that the PT explanation does not invoke any external *force* that acts on the acquisition process such as could possibly be assumed for the effect of motivation on SLA or the wind in the example of the rustling leaves. Instead, the PT-style explanation is based on a *limitation* of certain processes required for SLA.

Explanations that are based on limitations are known as 'explanations by constraint' (see Lange, 2018). These kinds of explanations 'are "non-causal" because they do not work by supplying information about a given event's causal history or, more broadly about the world's network of causal relations'. An explanation by constraint 'works instead … by showing how the fact to be explained could not have been otherwise' (p. 5).

Several examples of explanations by constraint are based on the famous 'square-cube law' first described by Galileo Galilei (1638). The square-cube law shows that as a shape grows in size, its volume grows faster than its surface area. For instance, if you double the diameter of a sphere, its surface area will increase fourfold while its volume will increase eightfold. This principle has been applied to explaining phenomena in several sciences.

One set of examples has been discussed in biomechanics. Biologists wondered why evolution has not increased the size of animals by large factors – for instance, why evolution has not increased the size of a mouse to that of an elephant (Haldane, 1926). Referring to the square-cube law, biologists and geneticists, including Haldane (1926), reasoned that scaling up an animal by a large proportion (say 100), would immensely reduce its muscular strength because the cross-section of its muscles would increase by the square of the scaling factor (i.e. $100 \times 100 = 10,000$), whereas the mass would increase by the cube of the scaling factor (i.e. $100 \times 100 \times 100 = 1,000,000$). This would lead to severe problems for the cardiovascular and respiratory systems of the animal. Also, the bones of the scaled-up animal would not be able to support it. Therefore, elephants require a fundamentally different body plan from mice. In other words, the way evolution can 'play' with the size of creatures is constrained by the square-cube law, and the explanation of the proportional differences between small and large animals put forward by biologists is an example of explanation by constraint. Other applications of the square-cube law as an explanatory principle relate to areas such as engineering and thermodynamics.

Obviously, the size and body plan of an animal are not predicted with precision by the square-cube law just because the proportions of its body plan are known. Other factors also come into play, such as the supply and quality of food. The latter are factors that are assumed to cause the growth of the body. In other words, they relate to causal explanations of growth.

Now, in the context of this Element on PT, it is interesting to consider how causal explanations and constraint-based explanations are related. Animals will not grow without food. However, no matter how much food they get, more food cannot beat the square-cube law. We can draw the following intermediate conclusion from this observation: causal explanations cannot override explanations by constraint. The latter constitute a condition that is valid for all external variables. It is for this reason that PT is built upon the fundamental constraint-based hypothesis that we alluded to earlier: the architecture of the human language processor constrains the range of forms the L2 learners can learn, and in which order they can be learned.

Let us add a little caveat. A reviewer commented as follows on the point of explanation: 'I do not believe that nowadays the "causal explanation vs constraints-based explanation" divide is neither so important nor so evident as it undoubtedly was … when PT was formulated.' We would like to comment that the issue of which kind of explanation (if any) a theory can generate has flared up in the Complex Dynamic Systems Theory (CDST) framework that has recently received a great deal of attention (see Section 4.2). Complex Dynamic Systems Theory focuses on external causes (e.g. Larsen-Freeman, 2020). We feel that it is crucial for the future of SLA theory development to be aware of these fundamental concepts from the philosophy of mind.

2.2 Constraints on Processability

In order to gain an understanding of the constraints that operate on language processability we need to look at the architecture of the human language processor. In the first book-length outline of PT (Pienemann, 1998a), the description of the architecture of the human language processor was based on Levelt's (1989) over-arching model of language production that emulated most of the empirical and theoretical research available at that time. Later research confirmed many of the basic assumptions of Levelt's model (see Wheeldon & Konopka, 2023). Levelt's approach covers all of the processes from forming an intention to articulating it. PT focuses on one section of this chain of processes: how intentions (ideas) get expressed through words connected by grammar. In other words, articulation, interaction, turn taking, and other aspects of language production are outside the focus chosen for PT. This focus of PT is also the focus of many theories of grammar, and we will see in Section 2.3 that a theory of grammar that is compatible with a theory of language generation is a very useful instrument when it comes to specifying testable predictions generated by a theory of processability.

Let us now move to an illustration of this particular section. Levelt's (1981, 1989) 'linearization problem' is a good starting point for that purpose. Levelt pointed out that speakers do not necessarily conceptualise the ideas they intend to articulate in the same order in which they are eventually produced. For instance, when one says *She drove off after she started the engine*, one describes two events in an order that cannot occur in reality. One must start the engine before one can drive off. But when speaking, this order of events can be reversed when the context requires it. Nevertheless, the events must be verbalised one after another. One cannot normally verbalise two events at the same time. The linearity of spoken language is a fundamental constraint on language production. When the things one has conceptualised and the way they are expressed in spoken language do not match one to one, several processes are required that mediate a 'translation' of the conceptualisation onto the linear channel of spoken language. We will look at several examples next.

When forming a message, speakers bring bits of the concepts that they intend to communicate into attentional focus and deliver them bit by bit to the 'grammatical encoder'. The other bits are kept in memory until they can be delivered to the 'grammatical encoder'. Levelt (1989, pp. 236–288) discusses the production of a simple declarative sentence similar to (3) as an example of several processes that are relevant in this context.

(3)   The child gives the mother two presents.

The intended message entailed in (3) (and illustrated in Figure 2) is created in the 'conceptualiser'. At this point, the message consists of the three referents *child*, *mother*, and *presents*, and the semantic predicate *give* (plus some information about the definiteness and number of the referents). In the 'conceptualiser', these bits of meaning are not yet expressed as words. Instead, the 'conceptualiser' operates at a purely conceptual level as illustrated graphically in Figure 2. For instance, bilingual persons would articulate the same conceptual contents differently in their two languages following the grammar and the lexicon of each of the languages.[3]

The different conceptual bits can be delivered to the grammatical encoder in any order. If the first bit is *the child*, an active sentence will be produced (in English) as shown in (3). If the first bit is *two presents*, this will trigger the production of a passive sentence (in English) – that is, *Two presents are given to the mother by the child*. Other grammatical forms can also be triggered

---

[3] As long as the intended message does not imply language-specific conceptual aspects.

Figure 2 Illustration of the meaning underlying the sentence 'The child gives the mother two presents.' (© Anton Dörner).

depending on the sequence of delivery of conceptual information – for example, *The mother is being given two presents by the child.*

When we take a closer look at what happens inside the grammatical encoder, we come closer to the core of PT. The grammatical encoder works in a series of so-called iterations. These can be visualised as the frames of a motion picture. As the frames move, the grammatical encoder carries out very fast and automated linguistic procedures. Let us assume the concept *TWO PRESENTS* (the conceptual information pictured in Figure 3) is delivered to the grammatical encoder. The first thing the grammatical encoder will do – based on an automatic procedure – is to search for the concept *PRESENT* in the lexicon. There it will find an entry for the English word *present* that includes the word's syntactic category (noun). This information is returned to the grammatical encoder as illustrated in Figure 3.[4]

As illustrated in Figure 3, the grammatical encoder uses the information about the syntactic category ('N' for 'noun') of the word *present* found in the lexicon to start an automatic procedure that produces noun phrases very effectively. As part of this process, it connects the category information (N) to the appropriate kind of phrase and creates a noun phrase (NP). Being a specialised

---

[4] The feature 'plural' is created after inspecting the conceptual material. This process is simplified here to keep this text readable.

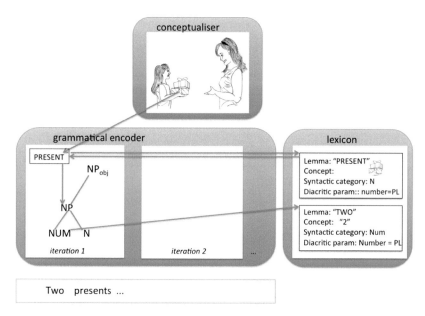

Figure 3 Incremental language generation (© Anton Dörner/authors). Adapted reproduction with permission from John Benjamins Publishing Company.

NP-procedure, it then looks for other elements in the conceptual material that modify the noun, and it finds the conceptual information TWO. This conceptual information again starts a search in the lexicon that returns the entry *two*, which is annotated with the lexical category 'numeral' (Num) and with the feature 'plural'. The NP-procedure attaches the element Num to the NP-node as illustrated in Figure 3, adds the feature 'plural' to the noun, and gets the morphological component to add an –*s* to *present*.

As part of this process, the NP-procedure also compares the features for number (= plural) attached to the noun (*presents*) and the numeral (*two*). In this case, it finds that the values of the number features match across Num and N. This matching process ensures that the two parts of the NP (*two presents*) agree in number.

As illustrated in Figure 3, the language-generation processes described so far occur in a specific order.

1. A lexical entry is accessed that matches the conceptual material in focus.
2. The lexical category of the word retrieved from the lexicon (N) is identified.
3. The grammatical encoder starts constructing a phrase (NP) based on the lexical category (N) of the retrieved word.
4. The grammatical encoder builds the constituents of the NP. The NP is also a procedure and one of its automated jobs is to check if the lexical features of the two parts of the NP match.

The language-generation process continues in the same stepwise fashion. After building the first NP, the grammatical encoder builds a verb phrase (VP) based on the lexical category found in the lexical entry for *GIVES* (i.e. the verb *give*), and connects the direct object (*two presents*) and indirect object (*the mother*) to the verb. Finally, the sentence procedure connects the NP-node with the VP-node and checks if the lexical features 'person' (third) and 'number' (singular) match across the subject-NP (*the child*) and the verb (*give*). In other words, automatic procedures are activated in the following sequence:

1. Word (lemma access)
2. Category procedure
3. Noun phrase procedure
4. Verb phrase procedure
5. Sentence procedure

In a more detailed analysis of the architecture of the grammatical encoder, Pienemann (1998a) added a procedure for subordinate clauses to this sequential list:

6. Subordinate clause procedure

Given that these procedures must be activated in the sequence shown in 1–6, they obey an implicational order. Each of these processing procedures constitutes a necessary building block for the next procedure: without word access (#1 in our hierarchy) no category information can be obtained (e.g. 'N' cannot be associated with the word *child*, i.e. #2); without information about the category (i.e. 'N') the grammatical encoder cannot construct the corresponding phrase (here 'NP', i.e. #3). The phrase also acts as a procedure, and it ensures that grammatical information is exchanged between the parts of the NP. Without the NP procedure the VP cannot be created, and without the NP and VP procedures the sentence procedure cannot be created, and each of these procedures also carries out the exchange of grammatical information between their constituents, as we will see in greater detail in Section 2.3.

This implicational order of processing procedures is the basis for predictions about the sequence of acquisition. PT's basic hypothesis states that processing procedures will be acquired following the order in which they are activated in language generation. As we have pointed out, this is the implicational order from 1 to 6 that is also illustrated in Figure 4. Because each earlier procedure is a necessary building block for the next procedure there is no other way in which it can be acquired.[5]

---

[5] The last statement echoes the way Lange (2018) characterises the working of explanations by constraints: '[…] by showing how the fact to be explained could not have been otherwise' (p. 5).

Figure 4 illustrates the implicational hierarchy of processing procedures for sentence generation by showing each of the procedures 1–3 and 5 in their sequence of activation.

When we apply this hierarchy to SLA, we need to bear in mind that L2 learners produce L2 utterances before they have acquired the capacity to implement all six kinds of processing procedures described in Figure 4. When they have acquired the capacity to implement the first procedure (lemma access), they only have the capacity to produce individual words, formulaic sequences, and holistically stored units. The development of the category procedure adds a key prerequisite for one capability: morphemes can be added to the word that can be inferred directly from conceptual information, such as the plural *–s*. However, at this stage, learners cannot yet build phrases, and therefore they cannot map lexical features between different parts of the phrase (as, e.g., in *all my friends* – with *all* and *friends* both marking plural). It is exactly this capacity of mapping lexical features in NPs that emerges as soon as NPs can be constructed (level 3 in Figure 4). Note that mapping lexical features involves the exchange of grammatical information between parts of a phrase,

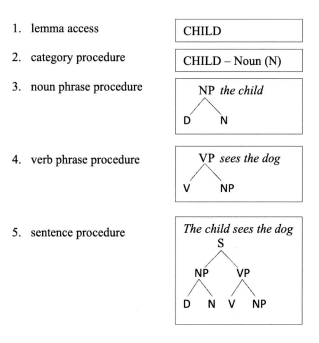

1. lemma access

2. category procedure

3. noun phrase procedure

4. verb phrase procedure

5. sentence procedure

6. subordinate clause procedure ……….

Figure 4 Implicational hierarchy of processing procedures for sentence generation.

but level 5 in Figure 4, the S-procedure, is more complex. We will see that several grammatical structures can only be produced with the S-procedure in place (e.g. third person *–s* and subject–verb inversion).

So what do learners do when not all the necessary processing procedures are yet in place? According to PT, they will map conceptual information straight to lexical material and add grammatical structures to their own intermediate L2 system in the order in which they become available following the hierarchy of processing procedures. This temporary simplification of target language-processing procedures (marked 'simplified' in Table 1) enables learners to produce sentences before the target language S-procedure has developed. These fundamental hypotheses underlying PT are illustrated in Table 1 as a temporal sequence (from t1 to t5).

Let us now consider an example of how sequences of SLA follow from the constraints inherent in the implicational nature of the processing procedures outlined previously. For this brief example we will focus on the acquisition of past *–ed*, plural *–s*, and third person *–s*.

As can be seen in Figure 5, past *–ed* marking relies solely on category information (everything can be found within the lexical entry for the verb), whereas plural *–s* marking (*two kid–s*) is based in the matching of the feature 'plural' in the lexical entries for the Num (*two*) and the N (*kids*). In other words,

Table 1 Hierarchy of processing procedures (after Pienemann, 2011b, p. 37).

Procedures	Time				
	t_1	t_2	t_3	t_4	t_5
S'-procedure	-	-	-	-	+
S-procedure	-	simplified	simplified	inter-phrasal ➤ information exchange	
NP-procedure	-	-	phrasal ——————➤ information exchange		
Category procedure	-	lexical ——————➤ morphemes			
Word/ lemma	+	+	+	+	+

Adapted reproduction with permission from John Benjamins Publishing Company

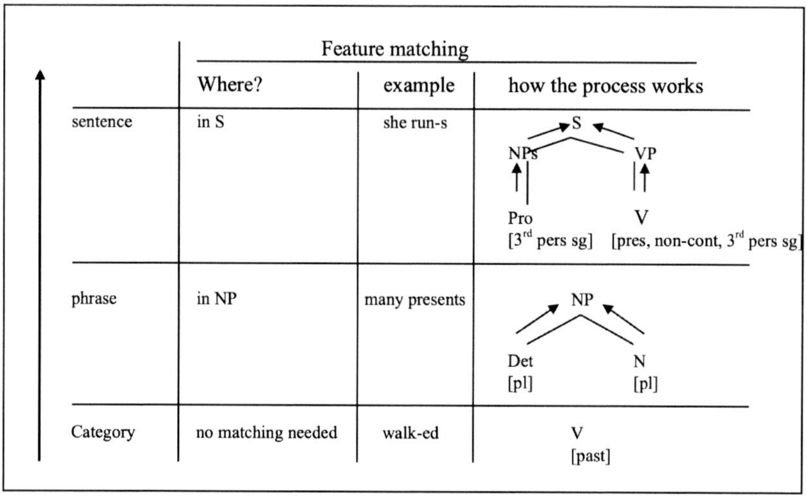

Figure 5 Three types of processes in morphology (Pienemann, 2011b, p. 35). Adapted reproduction with permission from John Benjamins Publishing Company.

the information 'plural' is exchanged between the numeral and the noun. This matching process is illustrated by the arrows that symbolise the upward percolation of the features 'plural' from the two lexical items and their unification inside the NP-procedure. In contrast, third person singular *–s* involves the matching of the two features 'third person' and 'singular' between the subject-NP and the verb. As illustrated in Figure 5, the percolation of the features goes all the way up, passing through the NP-procedures and the VP-procedure, and is finally carried out inside the S-procedure. Most importantly, only the S-procedure has the capacity to carry out the process of matching the lexical features involved.

The scenario that we have outlined so far provides a first basis for illustrating the explanatory logic of PT. Given that the category procedure is a necessary prerequisite for the NP-procedure that, in turn, is a necessary prerequisite for the S-procedure, PT predicts that past *–ed* will develop before plural *–s* that will develop before the third person *–s*. Next we will set out the formal framework for analysing L2 processing constraints for different grammatical phenomena and how these analyses and predictions can be tested in empirical data.

2.3 Implementing Processing Constraints in a Testable Theory

We follow the view about SLA theories expressed by VanPatten et al. (2020b, p. 2) in their introduction to the widely read volume *Theories in Second Language Acquisition*, where they state that '[a] theory ... ought to make predictions about what would occur under specific conditions'. In other words, the predictions made by the theory must be testable. This means that the theory must contain explicit instructions about the processes it entails and about the specific conditions that must be met for the processes to yield the predicted outcomes. Such explicit instructions are also referred to as the 'operationalisation' of the theory.

In this section, we take what may appear as a 'detour' via outlining some basic principles of Lexical-Functional Grammar (LFG) in order to illustrate how the transfer of grammatical information can be formalised in LFG. In Sections 2.6 and 3.5 we will show how these principles can be applied to other languages and how hierarchies of processability can be derived for other languages from these principles. It is important to appreciate that it is this seeming 'detour' of formalising the notion of transfer of grammatical information that permits the psycholinguistic notion of information transfer to be testable and transferable to other languages. Given that these fundamental functions of the language processor are features of the human mind, they need to be expressed in such general terms that permit them to be applied to any human language.

The things that are modelled by PT are specific to language processing. The language production grammar referred to by Levelt (1989) in his overall model of language production is Kempen and Hoenkamp's (1987) 'Incremental Procedural Grammar' (IPG) that models time-constrained language generation. Levelt (1989, p. 162) pointed out that because of its design, Lexical-Functional Grammar (LFG) is the ideal grammatical theory to complement IPG at the level of linguistic knowledge. There are several reasons for this. Most significantly, IPG and LFG share the assumption that grammatical encoding is lexically driven. This implies that the generation of grammatical structures begins with the lexical entry that matches the concept to be expressed. It also implies that the lexical entry contains a great deal of grammatical information that is used successively for the generation of the message. Moreover, the mapping of lexical features is a key aspect of language generation in Levelt's model and hence in IPG, and the mapping of lexical features can be operationalised in LFG through feature unification as illustrated in (7) (see Pienemann, 1998a, pp. 97–98 for further details). For these reasons Pienemann (1998a) used LFG as a shorthand version of IPG processes that formally captures key aspects of language processing.

In the context of this brief introduction to PT we intend to familiarise the reader with selected and accessible examples of the way in which LFG serves as a tool for operationalising processing constraints. The limited space available in this Element does not permit us to give a full overview of LFG and the full range of linguistic phenomena that can be operationalised using LFG. For a more detailed and yet introductory account of these issues we suggest the book-length introduction to PT (Pienemann & Keßler, 2011). In-depth accounts are available in Pienemann (1998a, 2005b). In this section we will focus on an LFG account of the hierarchy of morphemes we discussed in Section 2.2 as well as on aspects of English question formation. Both sets of phenomena will be used as examples in the discussion of other aspects of PT.

The original version of LFG (Bresnan, 1982; Kaplan & Bresnan, 1982) consisted of three components: (1) a constituent structure component that generates surface structure constituents and c-structure relationships, (2) a lexicon whose entries contain information relevant to the generation of sentences, and (3) a functional component that compiles all the grammatical information needed to interpret the sentence semantically. The architecture of LFG evolved as linguistic phenomena were accounted for in this framework. In the 2001 version (Bresnan, 2001), LFG has three independent and parallel levels of representation as shown in the top part of Figure 6: a(rgument)-structure, f(unctional)-structure, and c(onstituent)-structure.

Pienemann (2011b) describes the structures and processes shown in Figure 6 as follows:

> A-structure consists of predicates and their arguments – specifying who does what to whom. [Arguments denote the core participants in an event, including 'agent' or 'patient'.] This component is related to the lexicon. Functional structure specifies the grammatical function of constituents (e.g. 'subject', 'object' etc.). C-structure specifies the surface structure of sentences. To account for the structure of a sentence, all three levels have to be mapped onto one another. (p. 39)

In the example given in Figure 6 (*Donald chases a mouse*) the agent (=*Donald*) (an argument of the predicate *chase*) is mapped onto the grammatical function

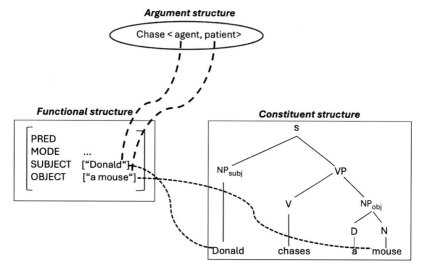

Figure 6 Three parallel components of LFG (Pienemann 2011b, p. 38). Adapted reproduction with permission from John Benjamins Publishing Company.

'subject' in f-structure. This mapping of a-structure onto f-structure describes an active sentence. In a passive sentence, the agent would not be mapped onto the subject function. Instead, it would most likely be left out or added at the end: *A mouse was chased (by Donald).*

Figure 6 displays the fully assembled c-structure. The curved lines indicate the exchange of lexical features. It is important to note that in LFG all c-structures are generated directly by phrase structure rules (see Figure 9). There are no intervening operations. Major constituents such as NPs are annotated for their grammatical function (e.g. 'subject', 'object', etc.). To exemplify this, the c-structure of the sentence *Donald chases a mouse* is shown in Figure 7. (4) shows a simplified account of the lexical entries relating to Figure 7.

(4) Lexical entries

Donald	N,	PRED[6]	=	"Donald"
		NUM	=	SG
		PERS	=	3
chases	V,	PRED	=	"chase" (SUBJ, OBJ)
		TENSE	=	present
		SUBJ PERSON	=	3
		SUBJ NUM	=	SG
a	DET,	SPEC	=	"a"
		NUM	=	SG
mouse	N,	PRED	=	"mouse"
		NUM	=	SG

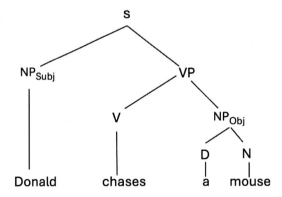

Figure 7 Constituent structure.

---

[6] The notation *Donald, N PRED = "Donald"* means that the lexical item "Donald" is a noun (N) and its meaning is "Donald". The second mention of "Donald" in double quotation marks is a shorthand notation for the semantic content of the lexical item described in a lexical entry.

(5) C-structure rules
    S   →   NP$_{Subj}$ VP
    NP   →   (Det) N
    VP   →   V (NP$_{Obj}$)
    V   →   chase
    N   →   mouse, Donald
    DET →   a

As indicated, the f-structure is a list of pieces of grammatical information that are required to interpret the sentence semantically. To illustrate this principle, the f-structure of the sentence *Donald chases a mouse* is given in (6).

(6) F-structure
    PRED   "chase" (SUBJ, OBJ)
    TENSE present
    SUBJ   PRED   "Donald"
    OBJ   SPEC   "a"
               NUM   SG
               PRED   "mouse"

One of the key principles underlying PT is that grammatical information must be transferred, and different kinds of transfer make different processing demands. Lexical-Functional Grammar serves to operationalise this principle. Above we alluded to this principle for a preliminary explanation of the order of acquisition found in different classes of morphemes that we refer to as 'lexical', 'phrasal', and 'inter-phrasal' morphemes, each of which requires a different kind of processing procedure (see Figure 5). In Section 2.2 the difference between these three types of morphemes was set out on the basis of the processing procedures (e.g. NP or S) required for the insertion of these morphemes. Using a simplified LFG formalism, we can now characterise more precisely the different flows of grammatical information for each of these psycholinguistic classes of morphemes.

Lexical morphemes: Referring to Figure 5, we noted that past –*ed* marking relies solely on category information. We can now state this assumption more formally. In the grammatical encoder and in LFG, verbs are annotated for tense as can be seen in (4) (see also Levelt, 1989, p. 191 for the grammatical encoder). This ensures that the information on tense is contained in the lexical entry – leaving aside the details of the actual processes of morpheme insertion.

Phrasal morphemes: In Figure 5 we exemplified phrasal morphemes with the phrase *many presents*. We can now state that the lexical feature 'number' (NUM) is listed in the lexical entries for the quantifier *many* and the noun *presents* in a way similar to the lexical entries for *a mouse* in (4). The NP-procedure serves to map this information within the phrase.

Inter-phrasal morphemes: In Figure 5 we noted that the *–s* on *run-s* in the sentence *she runs* is an example of an inter-phrasal morpheme, as the features 'third person' and 'singular' need to be present in the lexical entries of both the pronoun (*she*) and the verb (*runs*), meaning that these pieces of grammatical information need to be mapped in the S-procedure. In other words, without the S-procedure this mapping process is not possible. We can now specify more details of the mapping of lexical features. As can be seen in (4), the corresponding lexical features are listed separately for *Donald* and *chases* in the lexical entries. However, it is only after the c-structure has been assembled (and *Donald* occupies the subject position and *chases* occupies its position in the VP) that the two pieces of grammatical information (about the lexical features) can be passed up the c-structure tree and be unified in the S-procedure as shown in (7).

(7)   Unification of lexical features in the S-node

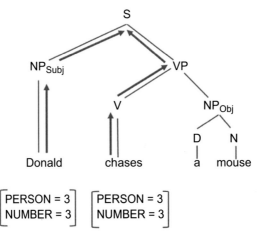

In other words, the PT notion 'inter-phrasal morpheme' classifies one type of morphological process that relies on mapping of lexical features across major constituents with the mapping occurring in the S-node. Using the LFG formalism permits PT to identify this class of morpheme in other languages as well – for instance, in all languages with subject–verb agreement. It is this kind of generalisability that enables PT to generate new hypotheses about orders of acquisition across different languages.

The PT principle of distinguishing different kinds of transfer of grammatical information also applies to other areas of language production, including word order. For reasons of limited space, we will confine ourselves to demonstrating this principle for an instance of word order relating to the marking of questions in English. Basically, English follows a strict pattern in the overwhelming majority of sentence types with the grammatical subject always preceding the verb – for instance, *Yesterday, we [SUBJECT] ordered [VERB] a pizza from Zia Lucia*. The most notable exception to this strict pattern is the marking of questions – for instance, *Where did [VERB] you [SUBJECT] order your pizza?* In these cases, the order of subject and verb is inverted (i.e. a verb appears before the subject). The c-structure of such Wh-questions is shown in (8).

(8)   Annotated c-structure of an English Wh-question

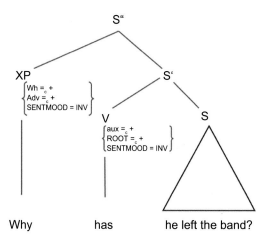

As shown in (8), subject–verb inversion is achieved by mapping the information "SENT MOOD[7] = INV" in the S''-node. The equation "SENT MOOD = INV" annotated to XP and to V states that the sentence is in 'inversion mode'. (For further details see Pienemann, 1998a, pp. 102–107). Mapping this information in the S-node ensures that the constituents XP and V can be filled only if XP meets the conditions listed under XP (i.e. that the word inserted here is a Wh-word or an adverb and that the statement SENT MOOD = INV is true) and if V meets the conditions listed under V (i.e. that the word inserted here is an auxiliary, that the clause is a main clause, and that the statement SENT MOOD = INV matches up with the same statement listed under XP).

Comparing (7) and (8), we can see that third person –*s* (an instance of subject–verb agreement in (7)) has in common with subject–verb inversion (8) that grammatical information is exchanged between two phrases within the sentence and that in both cases the information mapping occurs in the highest node of the main clause. Because of these processing similarities, the two

---

[7] "SENT MOOD" means 'sentence mood'. It is a piece of information that is connected to the constituent named XP as shown in (8). One can read the information appended to XP in (8) as follows: 'If the XP constituent is filled by a Wh-word, the sentence is in inversion mood.' This information is then checked against the information appended to the verb.

structures are located at the same level of processability even though one is related to morphology and the other to word order.

In contrast, no such information mapping is required for the production of affirmative sentences such as *You ordered your pizza* because they can be generated directly by the c-structure component or, alternatively, lexical items can be inserted following the order of conceptual structure, corresponding to the two bottom levels in Tables 1 and 2.

Within the limited space available for this brief exposition of key ideas underlying PT we have focused on a small number of exemplary ESL structures to illustrate how the transfer of grammatical information can be handled – in principle – using (a simplified version of) LFG. This account has formalised in particular different types of morphemes and word order related to the S-procedure within the processability hierarchy presented in Table 1. It also became clear that the LFG formalism does not require any transfer of grammatical information for the generation of lexical morphemes as well as for linear word order and (ungrammatical) Wh-questions without inversion.

In Table 2 we have extended Table 1 to include these insights about the transfer of grammatical information in the context of ESL morphology and word order.

As discussed, we have listed 'linear word order' (taking the following form "NPsubj V (NPobj)") in the line entitled 'category procedure' because this level is characterised by the absence of grammatical information transfer, and linear word order is one example of this. In the line 'NP-procedure' we added the structure "* Wh NPsubj V (NPobj)?" (i.e. *Where they drink coffee?*). A full formal account of how this structure is generated using the formalism sketched out above and which psycholinguistic principles place it at this level is available in Pienemann (1998a, pp. 172–178). However, here it is important to realise that the structure "* Wh NPsubj V (NPobj)?" is a linear extension of the structure that appears at the previous level with an added Wh-word in initial position. Obviously, this structure is ungrammatical in English. The line entitled S-procedure lists the two structures we discussed above: SV-agreement and SV-inversion. These two structures have in common that they require the transfer of grammatical information between phrases in the S-procedure.

Our argument is that ESL learners produce these structures because the language processor constrains them to produce these and only these structures. Learners are constrained because they lack the resources needed to produce the target structures. Given that at level 'category procedure' no transfer of grammatical information is possible, learners are limited to linear word order for the production of sentences, including questions that are only marked by rising intonation (e.g. *You are going home?*). At 'NP-procedure', the exchange

Table 2 Hierarchy of processing procedures: with examples of ESL word order and morphology (after Pienemann, 2011a, p. 37).

Procedures	Time				
	t_1	t_2	t_3	t_4	t_5
S'-procedure	-	-	-	-	+
S-procedure	-	simplified	simplified	inter-phrasal ──────────►	
				morphemes	
				example: *subject-verb agreement*	
				('he eat-s a banana')	
				word order:	
				subject-verb inversion	
				Wh Aux NPsubj V (NPobj)?	
NP-procedure	-	-	phrasal ──────────────────►		
			morphemes		
			example: *phrasal agreement* ('two dog-s')		
			word order:		
			(ungrammatical) WH-questions *without SV-inversion*		
			* Wh NP$_{subj}$ V (NP$_{obj}$)?		
Category procedure	-	lexical ──────────────────────────►			
		morphemes			
		example: *past tense marking* in English ('she walk-ed home')			
		word order:			
		linear word order in affirmative sentences/questions			
		NP$_{subj}$ V (NP$_{obj}$)			
Word/ lemma	+	+	+	+	+

of grammatical information that would be needed to produce subject–verb inversion has not developed. Hence, the only way learners can produce Wh-questions is to extend the linear word order pattern that is processable at that stage.

2.4 Predictions for Development Made by the Theory

Table 2 provides an overview of some of the key principles of PT. These principles lead to predictions about the sequence in which specific grammatical structures will be acquired – based on their processability. For ESL question formation the predicted sequence implied in Table 2 is as follows:

Structure	Example
1. NP$_{subj}$ V (NPobj)?	He go home?
2. Wh NPsubj V (NPobj)?	Where they drink coffee?
3. Wh Aux NPsubj V (NPobj)?	Where do they drink coffee?

A full analysis of ESL question formation based on the complete processability hierarchy predicts the following sequence of acquisition (thus adding structures #1, 4, and 5 in the next list), exemplified by structures with lexical verbs:

Structure	Example
1. Wh?	Where?
2. NPsubj V (NPobj)?	*He drink coffee?
3. Wh NPsubj V (NPobj)?	*Where they drink coffee?
4. Aux NPsubj V (NPobj)?	Is she drinking coffee?
5. Wh Aux NPsubj V (NPobj)?	Where do they drink coffee?
6. S comp NPsubj V (NPobj)?	I wonder where they drink coffee.

When we focus on equational sentences such as *she is strong* or *is she strong?* an analysis of the processability hierarchy predicts the following sequence of acquisition for ESL question formation:

1. Where?
2. *He is at home?
3. *Why he is at home?
4. Is he at home?
5. Why is he at home?
6. I wonder why he is at home.

The example for level 6 of the hierarchy (*I wonder why he is at home.*) contains an indirect question. The question *Why he is at home?* is formed ungrammatically at level 3, as direct questions require subject–verb inversion (i.e. the copula needs to precede the subject pronoun). The level 6 example constitutes a subordinate clause and an indirect question. In this function subject–verb inversion must not be applied in English.

In Sections 2.2 and 2.3 we also discussed the processability hierarchy for the production of morphemes and we found that the following sequence of acquisition can be predicted.

1. No morpheme insertion
2. Phrasal morphemes – for instance, past *–ed* (*they walk–ed*)
3. Inter-phrasal morphemes – for instance, third person *–s*

Stage	Phenomena	Examples
6	Cancel Aux-2nd	I wonder what he wants.
5	Neg/Aux-2nd-? Aux-2nd-? 3sg-s	Why didn't you tell me? Why can't she come? Why did she eat that? What will you do? Peter likes bananas.
4	Copula S (x) Wh-copula S (x) V-particle	Is she at home? Where is she? Turn it off!
3	Do-SV(O)-? Aux SV(O)-? Wh-SV(O)-? Adverb-First Poss (Pronoun) Object (Pronoun)	Do he live here? Can I go home? Where she went? What you want? Today he stay here. I show you my garden. This is your pencil. Mary called him.
2	S neg V(O) SVO SVO-Question -ed -ing Plural –s (Noun) Poss –s (Noun)	Me no live here. / I don't live here. Me live here. You live here? John played. Jane going. I like cats. Pat's cat is fat.
1	Words Formulae	Hello, Five Dock, Central How are you? Where is X? What's your name?

Figure 8 Overview of ESL developmental patterns.

A more extensive list of structures that have been derived from the processability hierarchy for ESL development is reproduced in Figure 8.

2.5 Constraints on Variability

Whereas the aforementioned processing constraints force L2 development to follow the trajectory spelled out in Section 2.4, they also leave some leeway for different solutions to the 'developmental problems' that we consider next. Learners face a developmental problem every time they try to express ideas for which they have not yet developed the means needed in the L2. For instance, as we noted previously, learners are initially constrained to use linear word order – mapping concepts directly onto c-structure. Therefore, ESL learners produce SVO structures at the beginning – including in questions (e.g. *he is here?* instead of *is he here?* or *he live here?* instead of *does he live here?*). In Section 2.4 we noted that English – like other Germanic languages – obligatorily marks questions through subject–verb inversion and that producing sentences with subject–verb inversion requires an inter-phrasal mapping of lexical features. However, this is a process that develops only later in ESL acquisition. The fact that an inter-phrasal exchange of grammatical information is acquired late causes a developmental problem every time early learners produce a question, because question formation requires a structure early learners cannot yet handle.

So, what do learners do instead? Different learners create different solutions to this developmental problem, as illustrated in (9), (10), and (11):

(9)   Is she staying at home?
(10) *She staying at home?
(11) *Staying at home?

Note that (9) is the target version of the sentence; (10) is a typical variant of (9) produced by an early learner. In (10) the learner leaves out the verbal element *is* that must precede the grammatical subject according to English grammar, thus avoiding the target grammatical structure that this learner is unable to process. In (11) the learner not only leaves out the verbal element *is* but also the subject pronoun. This 'solution' is another way around the developmental problem. Since the intended meaning of missing pronominalised subjects can be recovered from the context, (11) can be understood although parts of the sentence are missing.

This example illustrates two things. (1) The processability hierarchy leaves sufficient leeway for different solutions to developmental problems. (2) Both 'solutions' (10 and 11) obey the linear word order constraint that is imposed on the learners' language by the processability hierarchy. But the examples demonstrate that learners can select different developmental trajectories within the confines dictated by the processability hierarchy. The leeway for different solutions to developmental problems has also been referred to as 'Hypothesis Space' (see Pienemann 1998a, 231).

The range of options described for our example of a developmental problem also exists for other developmental problems along the processability hierarchy. One aspect of these options relates to leaving out elements that are obligatory in the L2 and that can be semantically recovered from the context. These include the following elements:

Linguistic element	Example
- Auxiliary	When she bought the car?
- Subject	Jim nice doctor. Work in small hospital.
- Verb	When they to America?
- Article	When she buy car?
- Preposition	When they go America?

Developmental problems also arise for the acquisition of morphology. As we noted in Section 2.3, English subject–verb agreement materialises as third person *–s* or as the forms *is*, *has*, or *does* of the auxiliaries *be*, *have*, and *do*. We also noted that subject–verb agreement develops late because it requires an inter-phrasal exchange of grammatical information. However, learners need to express concepts referring to third persons before they can process an inter-phrasal exchange of grammatical information. This mismatch of intended message and available processing resources creates another developmental problem. Again, the processability hierarchy leaves some leeway for different solutions as illustrated in the following examples:

(12) She eats a banana every morning.
(13) She will eat a banana every morning.
(14) *She eat a banana every morning.
(15) *She eating a banana every morning.

Sentence (12) is an example of subject–verb agreement and follows the grammar of English, whereas (13) through (15) exemplify different ways of avoiding subject–verb agreement and nevertheless getting the message across.

Utilising these and other options opens up a wide space for learner variation, all of which is within the confines defined by the processability hierarchy. In other words, the processability hierarchy operates across two dimensions. On the one hand, it constrains the development of L2 grammar in a way that results in staged development. On the other hand, it simultaneously leaves sufficient leeway at every stage to allow for different developmental trajectories. This interrelationship between development and learner variation is illustrated graphically in Figure 9.

Figure 9 illustrates the overall stages of L2 development and the leeway for different solutions to developmental problems resulting in different developmental trajectories (i.e. including path 1 and path 2) with path 1 leading to a less simplified target variety than path 2.

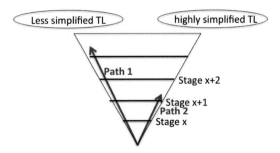

Figure 9 L2 development and variation.

2.6 Cross-Linguistic Validity

In Sections 2.2, 2.3, and 2.4 we noted that the reasoning behind PT rests on the following logic:

1. Which forms the L2 learners are able to acquire depends on which procedures of the language processor have developed at a given point in their L2 development.
2. The overall architecture of the language processor is the same for all human learners.
3. The way this architecture is utilised in individual languages is specific to those languages.
4. The order in which processing procedures can develop in learners for a given L2 is determined by the overall implicational hierarchy of processing procedures outlined in Section 2.2.

Therefore, the overall implicational hierarchy of processing procedures constitutes the basis for making predictions about developmental trajectories in different L2s. Initially, Pienemann (1998a) applied the hierarchy of processing procedures to a number of L2s, including English, German, and Swedish. It turned out that where these different L2s overlap structurally, very similar developmental trajectories can be derived from the hierarchy of processing procedures (e.g. for word order). And indeed these predictions were all supported by extensive empirical studies (see Pienemann, 1998a for details).

However, English, German, and Swedish are all Germanic languages, and they are historically very closely related. For instance, they all mark questions by word order, mostly by a variant of a constraint that places a verbal element in a position before the grammatical subject. So it was essential for the hierarchy to be tested with languages that are structurally different and that are historically not closely related.

In such a validity test we apply the processability hierarchy to specific structures of a second language. For instance, testing the types of morphemes discussed earlier in this Element for Finnish, a non-Indo-European language, we inspect the morphology of Finnish for instances of lexical, phrasal, and inter-phrasal morphemes. Considering the sentence *vanhoja karttoja ovat pöydillä* (*Old maps are on the tables*) the corresponding lexical entries are listed in (16).

(16) Lexical entries

Vanh-oja	A,	PRED	=	"old"
		NUM	=	PL
kartt-oja	N,	PRED	=	"map"
		NUM	=	PL
		PERS[8]	=	3
ova-t	V,	PRED	=	"are" (SUBJ, PREDLINK[9])
		TENSE	=	Present
		SUBJ PERSON	=	3
		SUBJ NUM	=	PL
pöyd-i-llä	N,	PRED	=	"table-on"
		NUM	=	PL

As can be inferred from (16), there are two sets of lexical features in the Finnish example sentence that need to be matched. The subject NP is marked for plural and third person and so is the verb that requires the affix *–t*. Within the NP the adjective *vanh-oja* and the noun *kartt-oja* are also marked for plural, each requiring the affix *–oja*. And the noun *pöyd-i-lla* (*on the tables*) is also marked for plural by the affix *–i*. However, this latter noun does not require any mapping of features with any other parts of the sentence.

(17) Unification of lexical features in the sentence *vanhoja karttoja ovat pöydillä* (*Old maps are on the tables*)

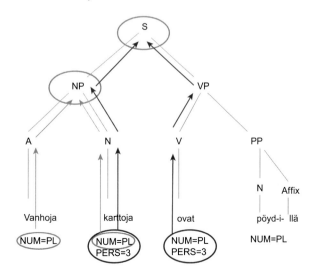

---

[8] All nouns are third person, but we marked it here for the sake of clarity.
[9] PREDLINK is a type of copula complement (see Dalrymple et al., 2004).

As illustrated in (17), the aforementioned sets of lexical features are unified in different nodes. The unification of the plural-value for NUM (highlighted with a blue oval and blue arrows in (17)) occurs in the NP-node, enabling number agreement in the subject-NP (*vanh-oja kartt-oja*) (*old maps*). In contrast, the unification of the values for NUM and PERS (highlighted with a red oval and red arrows in (17)) occurs in the S-node, enabling subject–verb agreement (*vanhoja karttoja ova–t*) (*old maps are*). In this context, the nominal affix – *oja* is an example of a phrasal affix but the verbal affix –*t* is an example of an inter-phrasal morpheme. And the nominal affix –*i* in *pöydillä* is an example of a lexical morpheme (in this context) because it does not require any exchange of grammatical information. Identifying the different kind of processing procedures associated with each morpheme allows us to infer the following prediction for a developmental sequence of these Finnish morphemes: –*i* before –*oja* before –*t* (for the given grammatical contexts).

A further aspect of the cross-linguistic application of PT concerns the way argument structure (containing semantic roles such as agent, patient, etc.) is mapped onto functional structure (containing grammatical functions such as Subject, Object, etc.). This mapping process was mentioned briefly in Section 2.3 where it was illustrated with the following example:

(18) Donald chases a mouse.

In this example, the agent (= *Donald*) (an argument of the predicate *chase*) is mapped onto the grammatical function Subject in f-structure. We also noted in Section 2.3 that this particular mapping of a- to f-structure results in an active sentence and that in a passive sentence, the agent would not be mapped onto the Subject function. Instead, it would most likely be left out or added at the end (as an Adjunct) and the patient would be mapped onto the Subject function, as shown in (19).

(19) A mouse was chased by Donald.

Pienemann et al. (2005) showed that the most natural and computationally least costly way to map a-structure onto f-structure is the one-to-one mapping of semantic roles onto grammatical functions as illustrated in (20a) and (20b):

(20a) Donald chases a mouse.

(20b)   chase   <Agent, Patient>
                            | |
                          SUBJ   OBJ

The one-to-one mapping shown in (20b) is the unmarked case of this mapping process, whereas in the passive sentence in (19) the mapping process deviates from the natural default as shown in (21a) and (21b).

(21a)   A mouse was chased by Donald.

(21b)   chased   <Agent, Patient>

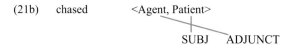

                        SUBJ   ADJUNCT

Pienemann et al. (2005, p. 240) argued that this deviation from the default requires additional processing procedures and it is therefore acquired later than default mapping (see also Kawaguchi, 2023, pp. 35–42). This observation adds one further building block to PT's processability hierarchy that will be utilised in Kawaguchi's summary of her research paper on Japanese SLA. Kawaguchi's research can be seen as a further test of the cross-linguistic plausibility of the processability hierarchy (see Info Box 1).

INFO BOX 1 THE TYPOLOGICAL PLAUSIBILITY OF PROCESSABILITY THEORY FOR JAPANESE L2
Satomi Kawaguchi

What this study is about and why it is important

This study was designed as a test of PT-based predictions for the development of morphological markers in Japanese as a second language. PT assumes the following universal sequence of morphological markers based on their processability:

(1) lexical morphemes
(2) phrasal morphemes
(3) inter-phrasal morphemes.

This hierarchy was applied to Japanese and tested using data from a three-year longitudinal study involving an English L1 student learning Japanese L2 at an Australian university.

Research design

Conversational data were collected from an Australian learner of Japanese as L2. The aforementioned PT hierarchy for morphology was applied to Japanese yielding the following predictions for a developmental sequence:

INFO BOX 1 (cont.)

Stage	Structure	Example	
(1)	Lexical: Verb Inflection		
	Vstem-POL PRES	*tabe-masu*	'(I/you/they/etc.) eat'
	Vstem-POL PAST	*tabe-mashita*	'(I/you/they/etc.) ate'
	Vstem-POL NEG	*tabe-masen*	'(I/you/they/etc.) do not eat'
	Vstem-POL NEG-PAST	*tabe-masen-deshita*	'(I/you/they/etc.) did not eat'
(2)	Phrasal: V-*te* V		
	V-*te* PROG	*tabe-te imasu*	'(I/you/they/etc.) am/are eating'
	V-*te* REQUEST	*tabe-te kudasai*	'Please eat'
(3)	Inter-phrasal:		
	Passive	*neko-ga sakana-ni tabe-rare-ta* fish-NOM cat-DAT eat-PASS-PAST 'The fish was eaten by the cat.'	
	Causative	*okaasan-ga kodomo-ni yasai-o tabe-sase-ta* mother-NOM child-DAT vegetables-ACC eat-CAUS-PAST 'The mother made the child eat vegetables.'	
	Benefactive	*musume-ga okaasan-ni kohii-o tukut-te age-ta* daughter-NOM mother-DAT coffee-ACC make BENE-PAST 'The daughter made coffee for (the benefit of) the mother.'	

In Japanese, lexical procedures involve verbal inflection where the inflectional morpheme is attached to the verb stem to mark information such as tense. This enables the learner to produce the structures listed under (1).

In Japanese, the verb may combine with another verb – for instance, *tabe-te imasu* (see (2)). This construction requires the morpheme –*te* to be attached to the first verb stem (*tabe–*), and the insertion of –*te*, in turn, requires information unification between the two verbs (i.e. '*tabe–*' and '*imasu*'). This kind of unification process occurs at the phrasal level, thus classifying –*te* insertion as a phrasal process.

INFO BOX 1 (cont.)

The passive construction requires unification of information from different sources within a sentence. Consider the example of a passive construction given under (3):

sakana-ga neko-ni tabe-rare-ta
fish-NOM cat-DAT eat-PASS-PAST
'The fish was eaten by the cat.'

In this sentence, the passive verbal suffix, *–rare*, is added to the verb stem *tabe*, and this requires the appropriate markings of the noun phrases:

- *Sakana* ('fish') is marked with the nominative case marker *–ga*, denoting the grammatical function Subject and the patient role in this context (i.e. in the presence of the passive marker *–rare*).
- *Neko* ('cat') is marked with the dative case marker *–ni*, denoting the agent role in this context.

This process requires information unification between the verb phrase and the noun phrases. Therefore, *–rare* is an inter-phrasal morpheme.

A distributional analysis was carried out for the longitudinal data using the hypothesised developmental sequence as a matrix.

Results

Table 3 gives an overview of the distributional analysis.

Applying PT's emergence criterion to the data, the learner's grammatical development showed a clear implicational pattern (indicated by the dotted line) that confirms our hypothesis: 1st lexical morpheme, 2nd phrasal morpheme, 3rd inter-phrasal morpheme.

Things to consider

The acquisition of Japanese L2 stages has been investigated extensively in child L2, adult L2, and bilingual first language acquisition. Kawaguchi (2023) reviews major PT-based Japanese studies. Kawaguchi (2010) is a major study of Japanese as an L2. These studies empirically support the language-specific predictions derived from PT.

Table 3 Longitudinal study of Lyn's acquisition of Japanese (Di Biase & Kawaguchi 2002, reproduction with permission from Sage Publications)

Interview number	1	2	3	4	5	6	7	8	9	10	11	12	13
Date	3/96	4/96	5/96	9/96	3/97	5/97	5/97	8/97	11/97	4/98	6/98	9/98	11/98
Interphrasal													
Passive	0	0	0	0	0	0	0	0	0	1/0/0	0/0/1	0/2/0	0
Causative	0	0	0	0	0	0	0	0	0	0	3/1/0	0	0
Benefactive	0	0	0	0	0	0/2/0	0	0	1/0/0	1/0/0	0/1/0	0	3/2/0
Phrasal													
Vte-PROG	0	0	0	6	2	0	2	1	1	4	2	4	5
Vte-V	0	0	0	0	0	4	0	0	1	5	1	3	6
Lexical													
Vstem-POL→PRES	9	18	0	11	17	2	4	5	23	13	13	16	15
Vstem-POL→PAST	0	1	12	12	2	20	12	2	10	20	8	20	16
Vstem-POL→NEG	0	0	0	2	3	0	1	1	1	2	5	3	4
Vstem-POL→NEG—PAST	0	0	0	0	0	0	0	0	1	3	0	1	4

It is worth noting in this context that these principles have also been applied to the acquisition of a number of typologically different languages, such as Arabic (Mansouri, 2005), Modern Standard Chinese (Zhang, 2005), or Italian (Di Biase & Kawaguchi, 2002) (see Pienemann, 2005a, pp. 61–65 and Dyson & Håkansson, 2017, pp. 79–102 for further details).

2.7 Postscript: The Quine–Duhem Thesis and Galileo Galilei

We stated the following at the beginning of Section 2.3:

> We follow the view about SLA theories expressed by VanPatten et al., (2020b, 2) … [who] state that '[a] theory […] ought to make predictions about what would occur under specific conditions'. In other words, the predictions made by the theory must be testable.

In the preceding sections we have outlined how PT can be tested. Nevertheless, it has turned out in recent years that advocates of different theories may talk at cross purposes when it comes to testing predictions made by their theories. A prime example of this is the debate about developmental sequences in SLA. Obviously, one of the key hypotheses of PT is that learners will develop the second language stepwise, following stages of grammatical development that are due to constraints the human language processor imposes on the development of the L2.

de Bot et al. (2007) put forward the opposite view that there are no steady developmental sequences. Their view rests on two main arguments. (1) They present empirical data from longitudinal studies and claim that accuracy scores go up and down over the observational period and do not follow a staged pattern. (2) They claim that that SLA is a complex dynamic system in which '[…] all variables are interrelated, and therefore changes in one variable will have an impact on all other variables that are part of the system' (de Bot et al., 2007, p. 8). Therefore, they argue that '[…] any account that focuses on one aspect only cannot but provide a gross oversimplification of reality' (de Bot et al., 2007, p. 18). In the context of the current discussion of explanation it should be noted that de Bot et al. (2007) view these 'variables' as 'causal factors' (de Bot et al. 2007, p. 17).

We discussed explanations by cause and explanations by constraints in Section 2.1. PT offers a constraint-based explanation of L2 development and variation. Like in the riverbed metaphor, the argument is that the processing constraints imposed on L2 acquisition delineate possible trajectories for the theorised features and their variants and – again like the riverbed metaphor – the design of PT is not aiming at an explanation of all factors involved in L2 development and variation.

In cases where two opposing views are presented (steady developmental sequences do or do not exist), the public press is quick to conclude that research results are contradictory. But do we have information sufficient to warrant such a conclusion? What is being compared here? In Section 3.7 we outline the research methodology that is part of PT, including a specific approach to distributional analysis and quantitative acquisition criteria. It is only after applying this research methodology that is motivated by the theoretical constructs entailed in PT that statements on the presence or absence of developmental sequences as defined in and predicted by PT can be decided on. de Bot et al. use a rather different approach to data analysis that may be useful in the context of their approach, and their research is based on an entirely different set of theoretical assumptions. PT does not use the trend line of accuracy scores referred to by de Bot et al. (2007) to determine developmental stages. Instead, PT is based on a set of acquisition criteria that are applied to corpora of learner data after specific distributional analyses – as explained in Section 3.7. This process requires that the corpora examined meet specified criteria in relation to their size and organisation. Therefore, findings from the two approaches cannot be compared one to one.

The tangential communication we see here is well described by the so-called Quine–Duhem thesis (also known as the Duhem–Quine thesis) that is summarised as follows by Turnbull (2017):[10]

> The Quine–Duhem thesis is a form of the thesis of the underdetermination of theory by empirical evidence. The basic problem is that individual theoretical claims are unable to be confirmed or falsified on their own, in isolation from surrounding hypotheses. For this reason, the acceptance or rejection of a theoretical claim is underdetermined by observation.

In its general form, the Quine–Duhem thesis states that empirical evidence cannot test a single hypothesis in isolation from its theoretical context. Therefore, one cannot use data analysed in one methodological and theoretical context to test a hypothesis developed in a different methodological and theoretical context. Concepts such as developmental sequences are not directly visible in any given collection of empirical data, even though interlanguage forms may be visible. Determining developmental sequences requires the systematic application of a well-defined acquisition criterion. In the same way, water molecules are not visible to the naked eye or even through an optical microscope. Instead, they rely on theoretical constructs that can be tested empirically.

---

[10] https://philpapers.org/browse/quine-duhem-thesis.

This comparison of the visibility or existence of developmental sequences with water molecules is reminiscent of Galileo's famous claim that several satellites (moons) circle around Jupiter. It is common knowledge that this claim was vehemently disputed by the Catholic Church, more precisely by Cesare Cremonini, a professor of philosophy, who argued that the telescope Galileo used in order to produce evidence in support of his claim might introduce artefacts that produce the illusion of satellites invisible to the naked eye (Heilbron, 2010, pp. 195–196).

In fact, philosophers refer to this historical case as a prime example of the underdetermination of theory by empirical evidence. Nobody could and can see Jupiter's moons with the naked eye. Any evidence in support of their existence requires auxiliary assumptions that relate to the interpretation of empirical data. Galileo's claim was based on the then current geometrical optics that included complex mathematical calculations and Galileo's own technical improvements of the freshly invented refracting telescope. In other words, Galileo's astronomical claims were embedded in a host of hypotheses and assumptions, and they were not related to direct observation with the naked eye. His claim would have needed to be considered in the context of all of these hypotheses and assumptions. However, it was this context that Cremonini argued against from his own philosophical position in an *a priori* manner rather than either testing the contended claims in their theoretical context or examining the applicability of the auxiliary hypotheses including geometrical optics, mathematical calculations, and the refracting telescope.

Obviously, science later produced massive evidence in support of Galileo's hypotheses and assumptions, including an approach to the icy surface of Jupiter's moon Europa by the Galileo spacecraft in 1998 and an even closer approach by the Juno spacecraft in 2022.[11] It is equally obvious that the circumstances for scientific practice have also changed dramatically. However, as Turnbull (2018, p. 1) points out, we 'should […] care about [the] underdetermination [of theory by empirical evidence, MP & AL] because it impacts scientists in their practice'.

3 Main Branches of Research

3.1 Production and Comprehension

Most of the research within the PT framework focuses on the development of learners' L2 speech production and the underlying processes that enable the

---

[11] www.jpl.nasa.gov/news/nasas-juno-shares-first-image-from-flyby-of-jupiters-moon-europa; https://manyworlds.space/2022/09/30/the-juno-spacecraft-images-jupiters-moon-europa-as-it-speeds-past.

learners to produce increasingly complex utterances. A core question that has only recently been addressed in more detail is whether PT can also be applied to comprehension: do the mechanisms involved in L2 speech production, as introduced in Section 2.2, also play a role in L2 comprehension? Or do (L2) production and (L2) comprehension rely on entirely distinct mechanisms?

We contend that (L2) production and (L2) comprehension are not based on entirely distinct processes. Consistent with recent psycholinguistic insights on sentence processing (e.g. Kempen et al., 2012; Segaert et al., 2012; Gambi & Pickering, 2017), we claim that some of the key mechanisms involved in production also play a role in the comprehension process. Within the PT framework, we are mainly interested in how grammar is processed in production and comprehension. There is evidence that both processes occur in the same cognitive domain – that is, in a so-called shared coder (Kempen et al., 2012). Drawing on these insights, we argue that in L2 acquisition, there also exists a shared syntactic coder and that this coder develops stepwise in the acquisition process. Therefore, we propose that there are shared processes in grammar processing in both production and comprehension.

However, this does not mean that production and comprehension are based on exactly the same mechanisms. One major difference concerns the direction of the information flow. Consider the sentence in example (22).

(22)   Yesterday, John cooked pasta.

In speech production, we transform our intention about what we wish to communicate – in this case, that a person named John cooked pasta at a particular point in the past – into a (hopefully) well-formed utterance. In comprehension, we encounter sentence (22), and our task is to decode the auditory signal to gain an understanding of the content of the actual message (who is doing what at a particular point in time) (see, e.g., Levelt, 1989; Hendriks, 2014). Importantly, in comprehension, we do not rely solely on grammatical processing: we can make use of other cues, including lexical or semantic information as well as non-linguistic cues.

The potential use of lexical information is exemplified by the sentence in (22). Both the adverb *yesterday* and the past *–ed* morpheme in *cooked* indicate that the event occurred in the past. In order to understand the meaning of the utterance, the past *–ed* morpheme does not necessarily have to be processed, as the information regarding time is supplied by the adverb (e.g. VanPatten, 2020). Semantic information relates, among others, to the plausibility of an event. For instance, the event expressed in the sentence *The cat was eaten by the mouse* is highly unlikely, whereas an interpretation that reverses the roles of the two participants (as in *The cat ate the mouse*) yields a plausible sentence. Therefore, it is possible that we interpret the sentence based on the plausibility of the event, thus relying on semantic information. Lastly, non-linguistic cues, such as gestures, can also aid in the comprehension of an utterance. Studies have shown that using gestures that accompany speech, like pointing to an apple when saying the word *apple*, assists in message decoding and thus facilitates comprehension (e.g. Beattie & Shovelton, 1999; Dargue et al., 2019).

Research on sentence processing has revealed that listeners frequently rely on shallow, or what are also known as 'good-enough' representations in comprehending utterances. Their interpretations are often guided by semantic cues and considerations about the plausibility of the event (Ferreira, 2003; Christianson et al., 2006; Ferreira & Patson, 2007). For example, when encountering a passive construction, as in (23), individuals are sometimes tricked by its implausibility and understand the sentence in its active form (*The mouse ate the cheese*) (Ferreira, 2003).

(23) The mouse was eaten by the cheese.

To account for the observation that both syntactic and semantic information are utilised in comprehension and to model their relationship, Karimi and Ferreira (2016) proposed a dual-pathway system in the architecture of language processing. They argued that there are two routes in human sentence processing: the semantic route and the syntactic route. These two routes are illustrated by the sailing boat and the diver in Figure 10. The semantic route, symbolised by the sailing boat, is

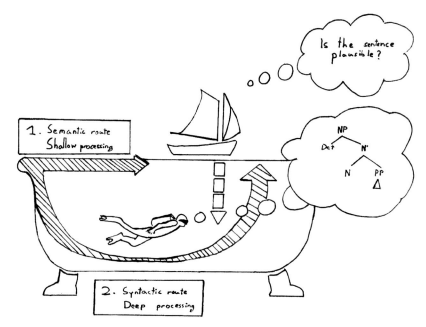

Figure 10 Two routes in sentence processing (© Anton Dörner).

relatively fast, as it takes into account semantic cues, such as the plausibility of the expressed event. However, the drawback of the semantic route is that it is shallow because it ignores other available cues such as grammatical information and, as a result, the interpretation it generates may lack accuracy. If we again consider the implausible passive sentence in (23), the interpretation created by the semantic route would be *The mouse ate the cheese*. On the other hand, the syntactic route, represented by the diver in Figure 10, is more accurate but involves a longer processing time, as the utterance is decoded in its syntactic details. Processing the sentence in (23) via the syntactic route provides the correct (even though implausible) interpretation that it is the cheese that ate the mouse. In this case, the sentence is processed syntactically, a process that is not affected by considerations about the plausibility of the interpretation.

In full comprehension, the semantic route (represented by the sailing boat) creates an interim interpretation of the sentence based on its plausibility, which is then compared for accuracy with the output of the syntactic route (depicted by the diver). In situations where sentence processing takes place rapidly, such as during a conversation, individuals may simply rely on the output of the semantic route. The claims proposed by Karimi and Ferreira are supported by studies such as the ones by Poesio et al. (2006), Christianson et al. (2010), or Cook (2014).

Lenzing (2021) applies these insights from human sentence processing to L2 comprehension. She argues that, in principle, the same processing procedures that are involved in the L2 speech production process are also used in L2 comprehension. As outlined in Section 2.2, one of the central tenets of PT is that the processing procedures required for speech production are acquired stepwise. At the beginning of the L2 acquisition process, learners have access to words in the mental lexicon, but have not yet acquired NP or VP procedures. In L2 comprehension, beginning learners therefore have to rely on the semantic route in L2 comprehension because, at this early stage, they have not acquired the processing procedures necessary for syntactic processing. As the processing procedures are acquired in a stepwise fashion, the syntactic route can initially not operate fully (Figure 11).

To illustrate this point, let us consider the passive constructions in (24) and (25):

(24) The cat is fed by the woman.
(25) Santa Claus is followed by the pirate.

The sentence in (24) provides the learner with semantic cues (plausibility) that aid in its interpretation. When determining who is doing what to whom in the scenario described in (24), learners can rely on the event's plausibility. Even though both participants in the event (*cat* and *woman*) are animate, it is far more

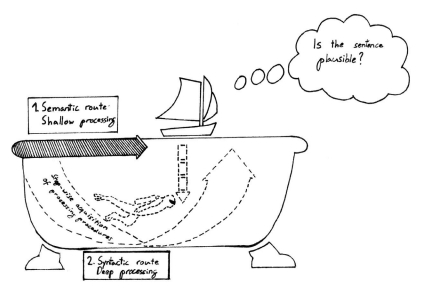

Figure 11 Sentence processing in SLA (© Anton Dörner).

likely that it is the woman who feeds the cat than the other way around. In contrast, the sentence in (25) lacks (real world) semantic cues that could facilitate the comprehension process. In this case, both possible interpretations of the sentence (*Santa Claus follows the pirate* vs. *The pirate follows Santa Claus*) are equally (im)plausible. Therefore, the learner cannot rely on semantic cues but has to process its syntactic structure in order to arrive at the correct interpretation.

According to the model proposed by Lenzing (2019, 2021), the type of passive construction exemplified in (24) that provides semantic cues facilitating comprehension can be understood by learners at a relatively early stage of their L2 development, before they have acquired the necessary prerequisites to process the syntax of the construction. On the other hand, sentences like those in (25) are claimed to be initially comprehended in their active form (*Santa Claus follows the pirate*). It is only at a later stage, when learners have acquired the resources to process the sentence syntactically, that the sentence is correctly understood as *The pirate follows Santa Claus*.

Lenzing (2021) tested these claims in a study involving eighty-two learners of English aged between ten and fifteen years in a school-based context. The learners were at different stages of acquisition (stages 2–5) and had German as their ambient language. The study investigated the learners' production and comprehension of different types of passive constructions. These included constructions that provide semantic cues that facilitate their interpretation, as in (24), and those that lack this type of information, as in (25). The learners completed both oral speech production and comprehension tasks focusing on passive constructions as well as a reaction time experiment providing insights into their grammatical processing. The results showed that (1) there is a correlation between the learners' comprehension of passives and their production, and (2) both comprehension and production of passives correlate with the learners' PT stage of acquisition in production. These findings align with the existence of a shared coder in L2 production and comprehension.

Additionally, the study revealed that, in L2 comprehension, learners at lower stages (where they have not yet acquired the processing procedures associated with syntactic features of passive sentences) comprehend passive constructions that include semantic cues, as shown in (24). It is only when they have acquired the necessary processing procedures to process passives syntactically that they comprehend passives that do not contain these cues, as in (25). Thus, the study provides support for the claim that with the successive acquisition of processing procedures in the course of SLA, learners shift from semantic to syntactic processing.

However, the ability to process utterances syntactically once the respective mechanisms have been acquired does not automatically lead to syntactic processing in every situation. Similar to L1 speakers, L2 learners may still resort to semantic processing in particular circumstances.

3.2 The Role of Formulaic Sequences

As outlined in Section 2.2, the architecture of the human language processor constrains the range of linguistic forms that L2 learners can produce. We have argued that at the beginning of the L2 acquisition process, the learners' options to express themselves are mainly restricted to single words and formulaic utterances. In this section, we engage with the concept of formulaic sequences in more detail. We offer a definition of the term as well as a way to identify formulaic sequences in learners' speech samples. We demonstrate that despite their limited linguistic resources, early learners exhibit surprising creativity in communicating their intentions, and formulaic sequences can serve as a highly useful tool in this endeavour.

The creativity in early learner utterances is exemplified in Table 4. The utterances in Table 4 were produced by beginning primary school ESL learners in Germany (Lenzing, 2013, 2015). The examples demonstrate that the learners produce both elaborate, grammatically well-formed utterances (the utterances produced by C02 and C01) and utterances that are seemingly 'strange' and, from a target-language perspective, incorrect (the utterances *What do you*

Table 4 Examples of early learner utterances

Learner	Utterance
C02	What's your name?
C01	What do you like for breakfast?
C14	What do you eat?
	What do you elephant?
	(*Do you have an elephant on your picture?*)
	What do you Baum (tree)?
	(*Do you have a tree on your picture?*)

elephant and *What do you {Baum} (tree)?* produced by C14). We will return to these utterances and provide a more in-depth analysis in terms of their status as formulaic sequences. For now, it is important to point out that some of the utterances can probably not be understood without taking the context into account. This applies to two of the structures by learner C14 who produced them in the context of a *Spot the Difference* task, where each learner was given a picture with only five differences from another picture. The objective was to ask each other questions to discover the differences. Learner C14 produced not only the well-formed utterance *What do you eat?* but also the non-target-like forms *What do you elephant?* and *What do you {Baum} (tree)?*. The meaning of these idiosyncratic utterances can only be inferred from the context. The intended meanings of C14's questions are *Do you have an elephant (on your picture)?* and *Do you have a tree (on your picture)?*.

We argue that in order to fully appreciate the learners' creative potential, it is crucial not to adopt a target-language perspective when assessing their utterances. Analysing learner language from a target-language perspective involves a focus on grammatical accuracy. This, in turn, implies a negative stance on grammatically incorrect learner utterances: from a target-language perspective, these are regarded as errors that reflect the learners' lack of competence in the language they are learning. In contrast, adopting a processing perspective on this type of utterances opens a window into the learners' internal grammatical development. Processing in this context means to take the different processes into account that are involved in the L2 sentence-generation process as well as the constraints that L2 learners face at different points in their L2 development.

We argue that it is useful to adopt a processing perspective when investigating early learner utterances and, related to this, their production of formulaic sequences. The term 'formulaic sequence' has been defined in various ways by different researchers, potentially leading to misunderstandings about the subject under investigation (Myles & Cordier, 2017, p. 5). A crucial difference in perspectives on formulaic sequences exists between speaker-external and speaker-internal approaches (Wray, 2008; Myles and Cordier, 2017). A speaker-external approach focuses on formulaic sequences that occur in the language the learner is exposed to. This includes, for instance, collocations – that is, words that frequently co-occur in the language under investigation. For example, you are more likely to encounter the combination *salt and pepper* than *pepper and salt*. These speaker-external sequences are typically identified by examining their frequency of occurrence in (English) language corpora, such as the British National Corpus (BNC) (see also Section 3.7 for different notions of corpora).

Speaker-internal approaches, on the other hand, concentrate on the internal cognitive processes of the speaker. From this perspective, formulaic sequences are understood as psycholinguistic units that are stored holistically in the individual's mental lexicon and can thus be retrieved without much effort. Common examples of this type of formulaic sequence are the phrases/questions *How are you?* or *What's your name?*. An example is evident in the utterance of learner C02 in Table 4. However, what is important for our discussion is that a learner-internal perspective on formulaic sequences not only considers well-formed formulaic sequences but also takes non-target-like patterns into account, as illustrated by the utterance *What do you elephant?* (C14) in Table 4.

Lenzing (2013, 2015) reported a study that investigated the occurrence of formulaic sequences in early learner language from a speaker-internal perspective. She focused on the spontaneous oral speech production of twenty-four ESL learners in a primary school context in Germany after one and after two years of instruction. The data are partly based on a study by Roos (2007) and were collected using communicative tasks at two points in time, the end of grade 3 and the end of grade 4. The learners' ages ranged between eight and ten years at the time of the first data collection and between nine and ten years during the second data collection.

Lenzing analysed all utterances the learners produced to gain insights into their linguistic resources. One focus of her analysis was on the type and frequency of formulaic sequences in the learner data. Lenzing subcategorised formulaic sequences into formulaic patterns and textbook formulae. Following Krashen and Scarcella (1978), formulaic patterns consist of an unanalysed unit and an open slot represented by X, which is filled with varied lexical material. This can be seen in the utterances provided in Table 5, produced by learner C06 after one year of instruction in English. At the time of data collection, she was at stage 1 of acquisition. The data were elicited using a communicative task called *Guess my animal*, which involved learners working in pairs. The learners were

Table 5 Formulaic patterns C06

C06	**It's a X?**
	It's a elephant?
	It's a pink?
	It's a brown?
	It's a green?

presented with pictures of different animals, and one learner selected an animal while the other one tried to find out which one their partner had chosen (Roos, 2007; Lenzing, 2013).

In the utterances produced by learner C06, the word combination *It's a* seems to form a fixed unit. Learner C06 combined this fixed unit with an open slot represented by X, which is either filled with a noun (as in *It's a elephant?*) or with an adjective (*It's a pink?*). In order to provide evidence for the claim that the structure *It's a* constitutes a fixed unit, Lenzing (2013) carried out a distributional analysis of all utterances produced by learner C06 (see also Section 3.7). The goal was to investigate whether the data set contained any instances of structures that diverge from the question form *It's a X?*. She looked for instances where C06 either used different lexical items, as in *They are X?*, or omitted specific features, as in *It Ø X?*. The analysis showed that apart from different lexical items in the open slot, the structure *It's a X?* occurred invariantly in C06's data. Based on this analysis, Lenzing (2013) classified this structure as a formulaic pattern. This procedure was repeated for all learners in the study. The formulaic patterns produced by early learners were either grammatically well formed, as seen in *Is it the snake?* (learner C23), or non-target-like, as demonstrated in Table 4 produced by C14 (*What do you elephant?*).

The second subcategory of formulaic sequences is labelled textbook formulae. These are grammatically well-formed structures such as *What's your name?* or *What do you like for breakfast?* (see Table 4). In the study, these formulae also occurred invariantly in the learners' utterances, and, in addition, they were unambiguously assigned to specific units in the learners' textbook.

These methodological steps allow us to claim that both formulaic patterns and textbook formulae are stored as holistic units in a specific learner's mental lexicon. This means that a particular learner can retrieve these structures as fixed chunks and that no additional processing procedures are required in their production. Therefore, formulaic sequences can be produced at the beginning of the L2 acquisition process.

The comprehensive analysis of learner data in Lenzing's study revealed that after one year of instruction, the majority of learners were at stage 1 of the PT hierarchy. Unsurprisingly, the vast majority of the learners' utterances consisted of single words (77%). However, formulaic sequences also held a prominent position in the speech samples, accounting for approximately 15% of all learner utterances (Lenzing, 2015, p. 110).

After two years of instruction, the production of formulaic sequences decreased to 9% of all utterances. Simultaneously, the number of single words decreased and learners produced more SV(O) structures. This development indicates that as learners progress in their language acquisition, they become capable of using the language more productively. A similar development from formulaic language to more productive utterances has been observed in research on child L2 acquisition in naturalistic as well as in instructed contexts in languages other than English (Myles & Cordier, 2017).

3.3 Language Transfer

A long-standing question in SLA research is the influence of the learners' L1 on their second language. This issue is controversially discussed in SLA research, ranging from the claim that transfer only plays a minimal role (e.g. Platzack, 1996) to the position that it constitutes a driving force in L2 acquisition (e.g. Schwartz & Sprouse, 1994, 1996). A popular and intuitively appealing opinion is that the first language plays a major role in SLA. One potential reason for this perspective on transfer is that people tend to focus on the way learners sound when they speak and take their accent into account (Lenzing & Håkansson, 2022). We argue that when investigating the role of transfer in the L2 acquisition process, it is essential to differentiate between different levels of language. While we can indeed observe language transfer effects in the areas of phonology (e.g. Kautzsch, 2017) and lexis (e.g. Neuser, 2017), the situation is different for grammar – that is, morphology and syntax. PT-based research provides evidence that the existence of developmental sequences in L2 acquisition limits the role of transfer in the area of grammar. This view is not unique to PT and is, for example, supported by Ortega (2009, p. 34), who states that '[t]here is robust evidence that L1 transfer cannot radically alter the route of L2 acquisition'.

Within the PT framework, the interrelation between developmental sequences and language transfer is captured by the Developmentally Moderated Transfer Hypothesis (DMTH) (Håkansson et al., 2002; Pienemann et al., 2005). The DMTH claims that transfer is constrained by processability, which means that only those structures that are processable at a given stage of development can be transferred from a learner's L1. The DMTH is illustrated in Figure 12.

Levels of   L₁ GRAMMAR   Lₓ GRAMMAR   Lᵧ GRAMMAR
Processability

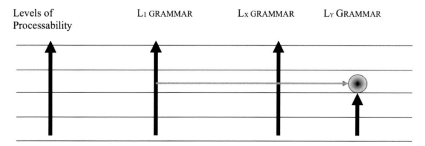

Figure 12 The Developmentally Moderated Transfer Hypothesis (DMTH) (Pienemann 2011a, p. 76). Reproduced with permission from John Benjamins Publishing Company.

As outlined previously, PT posits that L2 grammars develop in stages and that this staged development is governed by the constraints on processability (see Sections 2.2–2.4). These constraints result in the stepwise acquisition of specific morphological and syntactic structures of a given L2. The vertical arrows in Figure 12 indicate a learner's level of processability: the leftmost arrow denotes the PT stages of acquisition, and the second arrow illustrates the learner's L1 grammar. The grammars of their additional languages, denoted by 'Lₓ' and 'Lᵧ', are represented by the third and fourth arrow, respectively. The horizontal arrow in Figure 12 signifies that a particular grammatical structure can only be transferred from a learner's L1 once the language processor for the learner's additional language (Lᵧ) has developed to a point where the structure can be processed.

For instance, a structure that is in principle processable at stage 5 can only be transferred once the learner has reached this particular stage in their L2, even if the structure exists in both the learner's L1 and L2. This is illustrated in the following example of a German learner of Swedish (Håkansson et al., 2002). German and Swedish are both 'V2' languages – that is, in affirmative main clauses, the finite verb occurs in second position, as in (26).

(26)

This structure is processable at stage 5 of the PT hierarchy, and in both languages, sentences that do not follow the V2 pattern are ungrammatical, as in (27).

(27) * Dann die Frau kauft Schokolade.
    (Then the woman buys chocolate.)

However, this ungrammatical 'ADV SVO' structure requires fewer processing capacities than the V2 structure and is already processable at stage 3, when the learner has acquired the ability to front adverbs.

The aforementioned different perspectives on transfer yield different hypotheses as to which structures L2 learners of Swedish with German as their L1 can produce at different points in their L2 development. If one assigns transfer a major role in SLA, thus opting for a 'full transfer' approach (as, e.g., assumed by Schwartz & Sprouse, 1994, 1996), one would hypothesise that learners can produce V2 structures at an early point in their L2 development, given that this structure is also present in their L1. In contrast, the DMTH claims that learners are initially not able to produce V2 structures, as this structure is only processable at a later stage of development. Instead, such learners will produce either SVO or ungrammatical ADV SVO structures at this stage (see Section 2.4). Only when the learners have reached the respective stage of development can they (in principle) transfer the V2 structure from their L1 German.

The study by Håkansson et al. (2002) examined these competing claims with L2 learners of Swedish with German as their L1 at various stages of acquisition. The results provided evidence in support of the claim of the DMTH that transfer is developmentally moderated. The data showed an implicational development in the learners' acquisition of Swedish. Initially, the learners produced SVO structures, followed by the production of the previously mentioned ungrammatical ADV SVO structures. It was only at a later stage in their acquisition process that the learners produced V2 structures, despite the presence of this structure in their L1. These findings were supported in a study by Pienemann et al. (2016), who investigated the acquisition of L2 Swedish by beginning learners with German as L1 in a university context.

Further support for the DMTH comes from studies by Lenzing (2013, 2015) and is reported in Lenzing and Håkansson (2022). The studies examined the oral speech production of L2 learners of English with German background and investigated the extent to which language transfer could be observed in the learner data. The study by Lenzing (2013, 2015) investigated learners at the beginning of their L2 acquisition process at the primary school level, whereas the study reported in Lenzing and Håkansson (2022) looked at intermediate learners at the secondary school level. Lenzing (2013, 2015) showed that transfer only played a minor role in the speech production of learners at primary school level. The majority of their utterances consisted of single words and formulaic sequences. Structures that are common in the learners' L1 German, such as the V2 structure introduced above or the 'Verb-First' structure, as in *Fliegt die Biene in der Luft?* (*Fly the bee in the air?*) occurred either not at all or only in marginal numbers in the learner data. The same finding applies to the data of the intermediate learners: the two structures V2 and 'Verb-First' occurred only in isolated cases in the learner data. There were only three learners who produced more than one or two instances of these structures, as in *What wear you on the Mars?* (learner SM15). However, these three learners had already acquired the stage at which these structures are processable according to PT.

These examples demonstrate that the DMTH does not constitute a 'no transfer' position. Instead, it assigns transfer a selective role that is constrained by the processability of the given structure. In this vein, the DMTH constitutes an explanation by constraint (see Section 2.1), as the architecture of the L2 language processor constrains the transfer of grammatical structures from the learners' L1. With the DMTH, PT offers a constraint-based explanation for the scope of transfer in SLA as outlined in Section 2.1.

3.4 Stabilisation

One of the key features that differentiates second language acquisition from first language acquisition is the observation that L2 learners often do not attain native competence (Meisel, 1989, 2001; Long, 1990b). In a considerable number of L2 learners, development stalls long before native competence is in sight. Such a stalling in SLA has been referred to as 'stabilisation' (see Long, 2003; Pienemann et al., 2022).

From a PT perspective, L2 stabilisation is due to a particular interplay between L2 development and L2 variation. In Section 2.5 we pointed out that the constraints on language processing that determine developmental trajectories leave sufficient leeway for variable solutions to each of the developmental problems to emerge. For instance, when equational sentences are acquired at level 2 of the PT hierarchy, some learners produce equational sentences WITH a copula (e.g. *she is nice*) while others DO NOT INCLUDE the copula (*she nice*). Learners have been found to be quite systematic in their use of such variational features, and this systematic behaviour results in different developmental paths. In the case of the development of equational questions, two different paths have been found as shown in Table 6.

Both developmental paths satisfy the same set of processing constraints as set out in Section 2.3. In terms of variation, the two paths are differentiated by the presence or absence of the copula. In terms of development, a crucial feature emerges at stage 4 and is refined at stage 5: the positioning of the copula left of the grammatical subject. In English, this word order is a syntactic marker of questions. Given that in path 2 the copula is absent, there is no copula in this

Table 6 Developmental schedules for English equational questions differentiated by variational type

Path 1	Path 2
1. Where?	1. Where?
2. *He is at home?	2. *He at home?
3. *Why he is at home?	3. *Why he at home?
4. Is he at home?	–
5. Why is he at home?	–
6. I wonder why he is at home.	–

developmental path that could be placed in a position before the grammatical subject. As a consequence, the word-order-based marking of equational questions cannot develop in this strand and development comes to a halt. In other words, constructing equational sentences without the copula at stage 2 gets the learner on a track that ends at stage 3. In Pienemann et al. (2022) the emergence of this kind of dead-end developmental path was termed 'the wrong track pathway'.

INFO BOX 2 STABILISATION: THE CASE OF BONGIOVANNI

Howard Nicholas

What the study is about and why it is important

Pienemann et al. (2022, pp. 52–53) formulated the 'wrong track pathway' and showed 'how the internal dynamics of this process are able to tip the selection of an option in relation to the impending developmental problem in one direction or another' (toward or away from stabilisation). They documented five child learners of different L2s, none of whom had stabilised in their L2 development. What was missing was longitudinal documentation of a learner following a wrong track pathway. Bongiovanni is such a learner. His data was obtained through the longitudinal second phase of the ZISA[12] study led by Jürgen Meisel in the late 1970s and early 1980s and funded by the VolkswagenStiftung.[13]

Research design

We analysed Bongiovanni's data in relation to the supply or non-supply of the copula from thirty-three recordings over ninety-three weeks (see Table 7).

---

[12] *Zweitspracherwerb italienischer und spanischer Arbeiter; Second Language Acquisition of Italian and Spanish Workers.*
[13] Volkswagen Foundation.

INFO BOX 2 (cont.)

In Table 7 the first row indicates the number of obligatory contexts for the copula and the second row the proportion of required copula elements that were omitted, thus 1.0 indicates omission of all required copula in that recording whereas 0 means that there were instances of obligatory copula omission in that recording. A dash indicates that there are no relevant data.

These data were fed into the simulation described in Pienemann et al. (2022) (see p. 53 & supplementary material www.cambridge.org/Pienemann) to see whether the simulation could create a pathway that matched Bongiovanni's actual data. Bongiovanni's word order development was then investigated to see whether the hypothesised stabilisation of word order development at stage 3 could be established (Nicholas et al., 2022a).

Results

The comparison between the simulation based only in the dynamical aspects of L2 use and the actual data resulted in a good match. This result indicates that in addition to the previous findings that the simulation was capable of predicting pathways for learners who did not stabilise, the simulation could also accurately predict the trajectory of a learner following the wrong track pathway.

Bongiovanni's longitudinal word order data is presented in Table 7. The data from Recording 33 are consistent with data from all other recordings. The data presented in Table 8 show that Bongiovanni did not progress beyond stage 3.

This table provides evidence matching the theoretical prediction in Pienemann (1998a). The dynamical aspects of the L2 use of the copula predict not only whether a learner will follow the wrong track pathway but also that a learner who does follow this pathway will not develop beyond a predictable point on the separate aspect of word order. Thus the findings also provided the first longitudinal evidence of a definition of stabilisation articulated using Processability Theory as 'a lack of development (measured using the emergence criterion) within structural domain X, in context Y, and over time period Z' (Pienemann et al., 2022, p. 70).

Things to consider

Despite demonstrating how dynamical aspects of L2 variation constrain L2 development in specific areas, we are yet to establish exactly how the dynamical aspects of L2 acquisition drive development forward.

Table 7 Bongiovanni's rates of copula omission in obligatory contexts

Week	7	7	8	8	14	16	19	20	22	23	27	32	36	39	–	40	40
Contexts	0	3	2	1	0	11	1	3	0	1	5	3	1	4	0	5	5
Omissions	–	1.0	0.5	0	0	1.0	1.0	0.33	–	1.0	1.0	1.0	1.0	0.5	–	0.4	1.0

Week	42	–	47	51	57	59	63	65	68	72	75	78	81	83	91	93
Contexts	4	–	8	4	4	10	5	1	10	7	14	5	14	3	17	17
Omissions	1.0	–	1.0	1.0	1.0	1.0	1.0	0	1.0	1.0	0.86	0.8	1.0	1.0	1.0	0.88

Table 8 Bongiovanni's word order features in his last recording (Recording 33)

Stage	Single constituent utterances	Multiple constituent equational verb contexts		Multiple constituent full verb contexts	
		Plus copula	Minus copula	Verb constituents present	At least verbal elements missing
6					
5					
4				4	
3					
2		1	12	26	37
1	26				3

Pienemann (1998a) showed this interplay between developmental and variational features to be operational in many areas of morpho-syntax.[14] He also demonstrated that learners are consistent in their variational style with an individual preference for more or less simplifying solutions of developmental problems.

Why – following the logic of PT – do learners not just randomly choose different variational styles for different variational features? The argument put forward in Pienemann (1998a) is the following: every developmental trajectory develops from an initial state (of grammar). For equational sentences the initial state is NP (cop) NP. All later structures follow from that initial state. Pienemann therefore argues that the mathematical notion of 'generative entrenchment' (Wimsatt, 1986) applies to developing L2 systems.[15] As Wimsatt (1986) has shown, the benefit of generative entrenchment for developing systems is a massive reduction in the computational work that needs to be done. Rather than having to test every possible structural option each time the system changes, the mechanism of generative entrenchment ensures that only new features need to be added. By implication, old features are preserved. Therefore, early structural choices have consequences for later aspects of the developmental trajectory. Given that variational and developmental features are part of the same grammatical system, patterns of use of variational features also have the capacity to affect the developmental trajectory.

Naturally, the wrong track pathway hypothesis leaves open a number of unresolved issues. One of these unresolved issues concerns the long-term development of variational features in SLA. Although learners are consistent across different variational features in the way these are simplified, the degree of simplification may develop over time for each of these features. The crucial point of this developmental aspect of variational features is to determine the degree of simplification at the point in time when the variational feature (such as the absence/presence of the copula) interacts with L2 developmental features. In the case of the copula, this is stage 4 and 5 when a form of copula inversion is acquired.

Recently Pienemann et al. (2022) addressed this issue from the perspective of Dynamical Systems Theory (DST) (see Mitchell 2009; Feldman, 2019). Pienemann et al. (2022) demonstrated that the long-term development of variational features is subject to constraints inherent in its developmental dynamics. Due to the nature of these dynamics, the long-term development of variational features may be enforced either in the direction of a target-oriented

---

[14] The particular example of the copula was suggested to Manfred Pienemann by Malcolm Johnston (Pienemann, 1998a, p. 324).

[15] See Info Box 3 on generative entrenchment for further details.

use or in the direction of a highly simplified use. In the latter case, further development of the learner language may be impeded. Pienemann et al. (2022) developed software that generated simulations of the underlying dynamical system supporting this hypothesis. The simulations, in turn, were supported by comparison with longitudinal empirical data (see also Info Box 2).

INFO BOX 3 A QUICK SUMMARY OF GENERATIVE ENTRENCHMENT
Manfred Pienemann

Moser and Smaldino (2022, p. 5) summarise the basic idea behind generative entrenchment as follows:

> Generative entrenchment is a feature of developmental systems in which developmental events possess downstream dependencies … Earlier-occurring events involve both more numerous and more consequential downstream effects, which is to say they are more entrenched.

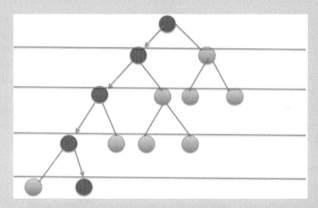

Figure 13 Downstream dependencies in generative entrenchment.

Figure 13 illustrates the concept of downstream dependencies in generative entrenchment. In Figure 13 development flows from top to bottom. At every level new features are developed. These are depicted as binary choices, suggesting that either one of the features can be added at the next level. In reality, there may be a wider range of choices. The idea is that as the system develops, features accumulate. Hence, early features remain in the system. In this way, early decisions have a great impact on the course of development.

Wimsatt (1986), the originator of generative entrenchment as a mathematical-philosophical approach to development and evolution, illustrates the impact of early decisions on later development with examples from embryonic development and evolution. For instance, when things go wrong in embryonic development, the earlier normal development 'derails', the more drastic the consequences are. Examples from evolution illustrate how early features are retained through generative entrenchment. For instance, with the emergence of vertebrates, the spine was retained as a 'design' feature for all later development in evolution.

Each time a new feature emerges in the development of complex structures such as language or life forms, such an innovation could theoretically be attributed either to a restructuring of the entire system or to a structure-preserving process that – by its nature – implies generative entrenchment. Wimsatt (1986) refers to the mathematical work of Nobel Prize laureate Herbert A. Simon (1962) in his calculations of the computational savings entailed in the structure-preserving route of development compared with a stepwise restructuring process. In his classic paper 'The architecture of complexity' Simon (1962) demonstrates that solutions of complex problems can be found more effectively when sub-problems are solved independently and the solutions are combined to produce the solution to the overall problem.

Wimsatt (1986) demonstrates the computational savings entailed in generative entrenchment using the 'developmental lock' concept as an idealised set of complex problems. Wimsatt refers to an imaginary combination lock consisting of ten wheels with ten positions each that he calls a 'complex lock'. According to Wimsatt, the total number of possible combinations on this unconstrained lock is 10^{10} and it requires 10^9 trials to find the correct combination. In the 'developmental lock' Wimsatt allows the problem solver to find the correct position of each wheel separately – following Simon's concept of identifying sub-problems – and to retain each of the solutions. The developmental lock requires a total of fifty trials at most (based on an average of five trials per wheel), resulting in an impressive computational saving.

On the one hand, generative entrenchment yields impressive computational savings. On the other hand, it constrains development by preserving earlier features. This is what was referred to earlier in this section as 'downstream dependencies'. In Section 3.6 we show that L2 learners of German retain SVO word order throughout the entire developmental trajectory, whereas L1 learners of German retain the initial SOV word order, and in Section 2.5 we pointed out that L2 learners retain the initial trend in learner variation rather than mixing variational features at random.

INFO BOX 3 (cont.)

Generative entrenchment also has implications for the initial state or in Wimsatt's wording, the 'innate-acquired distinction'. As early-developed features have downstream dependencies, the later-emerging design of the system depends to a great extent on the features that developed earlier. Hence, looking at the developing system from the perspective of a later state, there is no need to assume that all features that developed along the way were hard-wired into the initial state. Wimsatt (1986) illustrates this point with reference to the embryonic development of the species drosophila (see Wolpert, 1992). At an early stage of development, the larvae need to identify which part of the body goes where. Wolpert shows that the development of the body plan is not orchestrated genetically. Instead, the genetic code is limited to creating sensitivity to the degree of acidity in the larvae's environment. This information is sufficient for the correct development of the body plan. Wimsatt quotes this and similar examples to show that genetic information (contained in the initial state) is mediated by the environment, thus recasting the nature–nurture debate in the context of developmental constraints created by generative entrenchment.

3.5 The Case of Case

As outlined in Section 2.6, research within the PT framework does not only focus on languages that primarily rely on word order to indicate grammatical functions in a sentence. In English, the default word order is S(ubject) V(erb) (O)bject, as exemplified in (28). This means that the grammatical function 'subject' is typically realised as a pre-verbal noun phrase (*the mouse*), whereas the 'object' function is expressed via a post-verbal noun phrase (*the cheese*).

(28) The mouse eats the cheese.

In languages with more flexible word order, such as German or Russian, the same grammatical functions can occur in different positions in the sentence. This flexibility is illustrated by the two equivalent sentences in (29) and (30) for German:

(29) Die Maus   isst   den Käse.
      SUBJ   V   OBJ
      The$_{NOM}$ mouse   eats   the$_{ACC}$ cheese

(30) Den Käse   isst   die Maus.
      OBJ   V   SUBJ
      The$_{ACC}$ cheese   eats   the$_{NOM}$ mouse

Because word order is not a reliable guide to grammatical function in German, the two NPs in the sentence need to be marked for case, in the example in (29) and (30), for nominative case (*die Maus*) and accusative case (*den Käse*) (rather than the nominative case article *der*).

Over the past decade, researchers have engaged with the acquisition of case from a processability perspective, investigating the development of case in typologically different languages, such as German (Baten, 2011, 2013), Russian (Artoni & Magnani, 2013, 2015), Serbian (Di Biase et al., 2015), Hindi (Ponnet, 2023), or Italian (Magnani, 2019; see Info Box 4). Based on the underlying processing mechanisms proposed in PT, these researchers have established specific developmental sequences for both the morphological and syntactic aspects of case marking. We now illustrate the stages for syntax in the acquisition of case marking with examples from L2 German.

In his research into the acquisition of case marking in L2 German involving eleven learners of German with Dutch as their L1, Baten (2013) identified an implicational sequence of case acquisition in syntax that can be explained by the underlying mapping operations between constituent structure (specifying the surface structure of sentences) and functional structure (specifying the grammatical functions). Baten demonstrated in his study that at the beginning of the L2 acquisition process, learners start with a default stage labelled the 'all-nominative' stage. This stage is characterised by a default 'Subject Verb (X)' word order, where X can represent different kinds of objects or an adjunct, and default case marking in the nominative form, as in (31) (example sentence taken from Baten, 2013, p. 164, mapping processes added):

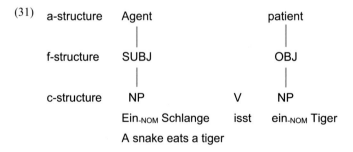

As depicted in (31), in these cases the mapping between arguments and grammatical functions is linear. Baten (2013, p. 121) argues that these linear structures are acquired prior to non-linear structures that are more complex in terms of mapping (see also Pienemann et al., 2005).

At a later stage of development, learners begin using case marking – that is, they produce accusative and dative forms; however, they still adhere to the default word order. This 'position marking' is characterised by learners assigning the nominative form to the subject that precedes the verb and the accusative or dative forms to the objects that follow the verb, as in (32).

(32) Er wirft auch seinen Stock ins Wasser.
      He NOM throws also hisACC stick into the water
      (Baten, 2019, p. 306)

Only when the learners have acquired the processing prerequisites for non-linear mapping between constituents at c-structure level and grammatical functions at f-structure level can they employ 'functional case marking'. This is exemplified in (33), where the accusative-marked object precedes the verb, and the nominative-marked subject occurs in the post-verbal position (example taken from Baten 2013, p. 217, mapping processes added).

(33)

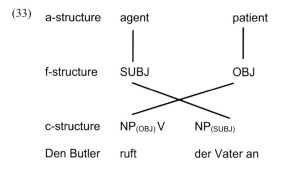

f-structure   SUBJ   OBJ

c-structure   NP(OBJ) V   NP(SUBJ)

Den Butler   ruft   der Vater an

The_ACC butler rings the_NOM father

This non-linear mapping between constituents and grammatical functions requires more processing costs and is therefore acquired at a later stage. It is one of the requirements for target-like German. The sequence of acquisition from positional to functional marking has also been found in other languages (see Info Box 4).

INFO BOX 4 SYNTACTIC DEVELOPMENT IN RUSSIAN AS A SECOND LANGUAGE
Marco Magnani

What this study is about and why it is important

This study deals with the acquisition of case and word order in L2 Russian. In everyday communication, changing the word order of a sentence is an important resource to enhance expressiveness. However, this type of

Info Box 4 (cont.)

resource often comes with a cost for L2 learners. In a language such as Russian, which displays great variation in word order, constituents must be marked by a complex morphological system consisting of six cases; otherwise the propositional content is at risk.

In this work I have adopted the framework of PT, with particular reference to the Prominence Hypothesis (Bettoni & Di Biase 2015), to account for the L2 development of case as a crucial means for learners to free up word order and hence express their discourse-pragmatic needs clearly and unambiguously.

Research design

- A cross-sectional study was conducted comprising ten learners of L2 Russian at different proficiency levels and from a varied L1 background (including languages with different types of case marking).
- Data consisted of semi-structured interviews carried out by means of elicitation tasks that were specifically devised for eliciting marked (i.e. non-canonical) word orders.
- Learners' production was transcribed and coded, with 395 sentences altogether being extracted for the analysis.

Results

- Beginner learners tend to overextend the default nominative case to all argument functions (subject, object, and oblique), and word order in their sentences is overall based on pragmatic and semantic principles, as in (34).

    (34) Anna   dat   kniga   mama
         Anna.NOM   give   book.NOM   mum.NOM
         'Anna gives mum a book'

- Intermediate learners can distinguish at least between a nominative and a non-nominative form; however, such case markers are only assigned on the basis of positional criteria – that is, the subject is located pre-verbally and the object post-verbally, as in (35). If an indirect object follows, it is usually marked by a general non-accusative case, as in (36), where instrumental is used instead of dative.

(35) Muzykant   kupil   trubu
      musician.NOM   bought   trumpet.ACC
      'The musician bought a trumpet'

(36) Muž   podaril   rozu   ženoj
      husband.NOM   gifted   rose.ACC   wife.INST
      'The husband gave his wife a rose as a present'

When, for discourse and pragmatic reasons, these learners wish to begin their sentences with the patient instead of the agent, they leave the constituent unmarked, and therefore produce sentences that sound ambiguous or awkward to the listener, as in (37) – with potential misunderstandings about who does what in the utterance.

(37) Butylka   kupila   medsestra
      bottle.NOM   bought   nurse.NOM
      'A bottle bought the nurse'

- Advanced learners can mark subject, object, and oblique correctly by nominative, accusative, and dative, and they can do so on the basis of functional criteria – that is, regardless of the position that constituents occupy in the clause, as in (38).

(38) Rozu   žene   podaril   muž
      Rose.ACC   wife.DAT   gifted   husband.NOM
      'The rose, to his wife the husband gave it'

Things to consider

- Within the PT framework, results confirm patterns identified in other case-marking L2s displaying a nominative–accusative alignment, such as German (Baten, 2011), Serbian (Di Biase et al., 2015), and Japanese (Kawaguchi, 2015), and the transitional paradigm from positional to functional case assignment has also been witnessed in studies on L2s with an ergative–absolutive alignment, such as Hindi (Baten & Ponnet, 2023).
- In the broader field of SLA, this study provides another piece of evidence that the syntax–pragmatics interface is particularly challenging for L2 learners insofar as case marking is more demanding in contexts which are marked pragmatically and syntactically.

> ### Info Box 4 (cont.)
>
> - In the area of language instruction, teachers of L2 Russian could use these findings to construct a more efficient syllabus reflecting the sequence in which case is learned, providing greater attention to students' communicative needs, and thus preventing the risk of potentially serious misunderstandings in real-life communication.

3.6 Comparing First and Second Language Acquisition

The reader will recall that the basic thesis underlying PT is that the architecture of the language processor constrains the way in which second languages develop. It is only logical to ask if this hypothesis also applies to L1 acquisition, because L1 learners also have a language processor, albeit one that is somewhat more under construction than the language processor of L2 learners. The unusual choice of words 'more under construction' refers to the fact that although both L1 learners and L2 learners need to develop a language processor for the 'target' language, L2 learners already have a cognitive system in which they can conceptualise thoughts as well as a first language processor. As we pointed out in Section 3.3, the L1 processor cannot be transferred wholesale to the L2. As a consequence, both L1 and L2 learners need to develop processing procedures for those aspects of language that we focus on in this Element on PT: morphology and syntax.

In Section 2.4 we stated that PT predicts the sequence for the ESL acquisition of word order shown in Table 9 and that this prediction is supported by longitudinal and cross-sectional data.

Some authors prefer a more traditional notation to describe the structures in Table 9. For instance, NPsubj V (NPobj) can also be conveyed as SVO. Strictly speaking, this notation mixes grammatical functions (e.g. 'subject') with constituent labels such as 'noun phrase'. However, the advantage of this shorthand notation for word order is that word order characteristics are easily recognisable for non-specialists. Using this notation, we will compare the development of word order patterns in German as L1 and as L2 in Table 10.

Table 10 summarises the findings from several longitudinal and cross-sectional studies of German as an L2 and German as an L1 (cf. Pienemann, 1980; Clahsen, 1990; Meisel, 1991). This work has been analysed from a PT perspective in Pienemann (1998a, 1998b), showing fundamental similarities and fundamental differences between the developmental trajectories found in L1 and L2 acquisition.

Table 9 ESL word order development

1. Wh?	Where?
2. NPsubj V (NPobj)?	*He drink coffee?
3. Wh NPsubj V (NPobj)?	*Where they drink coffee?
4. Aux NPsubj V (NPobj)?	Is she drinking coffee?
5. Wh Aux NPsubj V (NPobj)?	Where do they drink coffee?
6. S comp NPsubj V (NPobj)?	I wonder where they drink coffee.

Table 10 Comparing the development of German word order in L1 and L2 acquisition

PT stage	L2		L1
1	single words/ phrases		single words/ phrases
2	**SVO**		**SOV**
3	*X**SVO**		–
4	*X**SVOV**		–
5	X**V**S**OV**	+ *X**SVOV**	X**V**S**OV**
6	Comp **SOV**	+ *Comp **SVO**	Comp **SOV**

Children acquiring German as L1 start their language production with an SOV hypothesis about German word order, whereas L2 learners start with an SVO hypothesis. The initial word order of the L1 learners may at first glance appear surprising because in simple German main clauses the verb does not appear in the final position – as illustrated in (39).

(39) Er geht nach Hause.
     He goes to home.
     He goes home.

This is the least marked word order in German. However, the lexical verb does appear in the final position when the sentence also contains an auxiliary or a modal verb – as in sentence (40).

(40) Er ist nach Hause gegangen.
     He is to home gone.
     He went home.

In German subordinate clauses the verb also appears in final position – as in sentence (41).

(41) Sie ist enttäuscht, weil er nach Hause gegangen ist.
      She is disappointed because he to home gone is.
      She is disappointed because he went home.

Clahsen (1990) and Meisel (1991) demonstrate that within their chosen theoretical framework, all positions of the verb that can occur in German can be produced if one assumes an underlying SOV order and one single operation that ensures that a verbal element is placed in second position in all main clauses and that several additional operations are needed to achieve the same outcome when starting from an SVO word order.

Both initial hypotheses are compatible with PT, as the processing procedures at level 2 of the processability hierarchy merely constrain word order to be linear and demand that no grammatical information be exchanged in constituent structure. Both SVO and SOV satisfy this condition.

Hence, within PT's one set of procedures, there are two different developmental trajectories, one that is specific to L1 acquisition and one that is specific to L2 acquisition. First language learners typically reach the target language grammar that can be accounted for in terms of the position of the verb by an underlying SOV order, a verb-second constraint acquired at stage 5 in L1 acquisition and a verb-final constraint for subordinate clauses – acquired at stage 6.

In contrast, L2 learners start out with an SVO order and produce a sequence of structures as they increase their command of the target language. For these L2 learners, all of the intermediate steps have been shown to comply with the requirements of the processability hierarchy. However, they include a sequence of structures that are ungrammatical in the target language (marked with an asterisk).

Pienemann (1998a, 1998b) showed that throughout their developmental trajectory L1 learners preserve and modify the initial SOV-hypothesis, whereas L2 learners preserve and modify their initial SVO-hypothesis and that this conservative learning behaviour can be accounted for by generative entrenchment, a mathematical notion that we outlined in Section 3.4 in the context of learner variation. As mentioned there, the explanatory power of generative entrenchment arises from the great computational savings in developmental processes that are brought about by retaining structures that were 'discovered' early – in contrast to a constant restructuring throughout the development of the target language. Wimsatt (1986), the originator of generative entrenchment in its mathematical-philosophical format, demonstrates that this notion is capable of explaining a wide range of developmental phenomena in evolution, population dynamics, and society.

The issue that remains unexplained by these dynamics of L1 and L2 acquisition is why L1 and L2 learners start out with such fundamentally different initial hypotheses. The explanation Clahsen (1990) and Meisel (1991) offer is that L1 learners have access to privileged knowledge about language (via universal grammar), enabling them to infer the underlying word order of German from the input, whereas L2 learners only need to infer the least marked word order pattern from the input. In the case of German, underlying word order and the least marked word order pattern are not the same.

3.7 Methodological Issues: Data Collection and Analysis Procedures

This section focuses on methodological issues related to the type of data that are commonly used in PT-based research to test the theory's claims and to determine a learner's stage of development in their L2. The majority of research within the PT framework relies on the analysis of spoken corpora from one or more individual learners. These learner corpora consist of one or more individual L2 learners' spontaneous oral speech production data that were produced using the learner's own resources (e.g. are not read aloud) and were specifically collected for the purpose of a PT-based analysis. As the data need to exhibit specific characteristics in order to qualify for this purpose, these learner corpora differ from other corpora that are used in the field of corpus linguistics (e.g. Biber & Reppen, 2020 for English). In corpus linguistics, researchers mostly focus on large databases consisting of written texts or spoken language. They carry out computer-based analyses of this naturally occurring language in order to detect specific patterns in language use, based on the frequency of occurrence of particular linguistic items and their combinations. An example of this type of corpus is the British National Corpus, containing a large variety of spoken and written texts from different genres, such as fictional texts or newspaper articles.

With our learner corpora, on the other hand, we aim to gain insights into the interlanguage system of L2 learners at a particular stage of L2 development. In order to be able to draw valid conclusions about an individual learner's interlanguage and their developmental stage, the data we collect need to fulfil specific criteria. As we are mainly interested in the learners' spontaneous oral speech production, we need to create situations in which learners engage in meaningful communicative interaction and, at the same time, use their own linguistic resources to communicate their intention.

Second, the elicited speech samples need to include contexts for many of the morphological and syntactic structures present in the PT hierarchy in order to be informative about a learner's developmental stage. This means that we need learners to produce contexts for specific linguistic forms so that we can see whether a particular learner can produce these forms or not. As an example, if we consider the structures in the PT hierarchy for English as an L2, we can see that different question forms are indicative of different developmental stages. If a learner's speech sample contains Wh-SVO? questions, such as *What he say?* (Lenzing, unpublished data), located at stage 3, but lacks Aux 2nd? questions (*What does/did he say?*), it suggests that the learner has not yet acquired the stage 5 structure Aux 2nd?. In this case, the context for using this structure (an attempt to ask an Aux 2nd question) is present, yet the learner does not produce it.

However, if the learner's speech sample does not include any questions, we cannot draw any conclusions about the acquisition of the Aux 2nd? form. The same principle applies to other structures, such as the morphological feature third person *–s*. In order to draw valid conclusions as to whether the structure has been acquired, we need contexts in the learner's speech sample where the form would need to be applied (see Pienemann 1998a, chapters 4.2, 4.3, 6.5; Lenzing 2013 for more details).

A further concern relates to considerations about the actual number of the specific structures occurring in the data sample. The presence of one or two instances of a structure (e.g. the third person *–s*) could be attributed to a random production of the feature or a formulaic sequence (as in *What's your name*; see Section 3.2). Therefore, we require samples with a high data density. This means that a learner's speech sample needs to contain an adequate number (see below) of instances of the morphological and syntactic structures under investigation to be able to make claims about their acquisition. If a learner produces too few structures, the corresponding sample is inadequate for our purposes.

In order to meet these criteria, much of the data for PT-based research have been gathered by using communicative tasks. Communicative tasks exhibit the following key characteristics (see, e.g., Ellis, 2009a, p. 1): (1) There is a primary focus on meaning. (2) The task includes an 'information gap', necessitating the exchange of information among participants. (3) The learners predominantly rely on their own linguistic (and non-linguistic) resources. (4) There is a clear outcome other than the mere use of the language.[16] An example of a communicative task used in PT-based research is the 'Martian task' (e.g. Lenzing, 2021, 2022), a role play learners engage with in pairs. One of the participants is assigned the role of a Martian who has recently landed on Earth with a spaceship

---

[16] Pienemann and Mackey (1993) and Pienemann (1998a, p. 279) demonstrated the effectiveness of tasks in eliciting morpho-syntactic structures in a large empirical study.

while the other one takes on the role of an Earthling meeting the Martian. The participants are encouraged to ask each other questions about life on Earth and Mars. The Martian task elicits various question forms and declarative sentences and is suitable for learners at different age levels and different levels of acquisition (Lenzing, 2022, 2025).

The following excerpt of learner interaction in the context of the Martian task exemplifies that the task offers ample opportunities for meaningful interaction. It contains an information gap and compels learners to rely on their own resources in communicating. In terms of linguistic structures, the excerpt demonstrates that the task prompts various question forms from different PT stages as well as declarative sentences. In terms of question forms, in the example excerpt in Table 11, two learners, P19 and P20, produce Do-SVO? questions (stage 3), as in *Do you have my language?* (P20), Wh-Copula S?

Table 11 Example of learner–learner interaction in the Martian task (data: Lenzing, unpubl.)

Participants:
P19, age: 13, m, stage 5 (grade 7)
P20, age 11, m, stage 5 (grade 7)
Researcher (R)

P20	Ehm we need a story first what I when do you come from the Mars with a (…)
R	Spaceship
P20	(…) spaceship? and land here do you have questions or I?
R02	Maybe both
P20	Yes
P19	Yes
P20	Ok ehm ok I see you first then do you see me ok what's it?
P19	I am a Martian what are you? I never seen somebody like you
P20	Eh what language do you have? Do you have my language?
P19	I'm an English Martian
P20	Ok ehm ok I understand you ehm yes what's your question?
P19	ehm what are you doing on the Earth?
P20	Ok I can do a lot I can play with you I can fight with you okay I can play I can drive with cars it's on the street like this
P19	Ahh
	…
P20	You ehm speak from food ehm what do you eat? What do you can eat at the Mars?

Table 11 (cont.)

P19	Oh we're eat we're drinking water and we're eating how I can pronounce it? We eat paper you know? Paper?
P20	okay you have trees on the Mars?
P19	mmmh no it's metallic paper
P20	Okay very special

forms (stage 4), as in *What are you?* (P19), and stage 5 Aux 2nd? questions (*What are you doing on the Earth?* (P19)). They both also produce declarative sentences such as *I can play with you*, *I can fight with you* (P20), or *We're drinking water* (P19).

If we consider the example excerpt, how can we now determine the learners' stages of acquisition? The learners complete a number of different communicative tasks that focus on specific morphological and syntactic structures but do not reveal this focus to the learners. For instance, in Lenzing's (2021) study on L2 English, three different tasks were used. These included tasks that elicit different question forms, such as the Martian task, as well as a task that provided contexts for the use of declarative sentences and the third person *–s* as well as for Adverb-First structures, as in *At nine o'clock she go work* (learner G04).

In a next step, the data are transcribed and subsequently analysed for the presence or absence of the morphological and syntactic features in the speech sample. This distributional analysis serves to establish a linguistic profile of a learner and to determine their stage of acquisition. Applying this analysis to the complete speech sample of learner P20 results in the overview shown in Table 12.[17]

This simplified distributional analysis shows that learner P20 produces a range of linguistic structures located at all stages of the PT hierarchy. However, having examples from all stages does not necessarily imply that the learner has reached the highest stage of the PT hierarchy (i.e. stage 6). To determine their stage of acquisition, we need to apply an acquisition criterion to the data. In PT, we do not use accuracy as a criterion to determine acquisition, as research has shown that accuracy and development do not necessarily correlate (Meisel et al., 1981; Pienemann, 1998a). Instead of concentrating on *when* a particular target-language linguistic feature is mastered, PT focuses on the 'emergence' of the capacity to use these linguistic features. This denotes the point in time when a particular processing procedure has been acquired.

---

[17] For a more in-depth discussion of distributional analyses, see, for example, Pienemann and Keßler (2011) or Lenzing (2021).

Table 12 Simplified distributional analysis for learner
P20

Stage	Structures	No. of occurrences
6	Cancel Aux 2nd?	1
5	Aux−2nd-?	6
	3-sg s	4
4	Copula S (x)	2
	Wh-copula S (x)	3
3	Aux SV(O)-?	1
	Do-SV(O)-?	6
	Adverb-First	12
2	S neg V(O)	2
	SVO	35
	SVO?	3
	-ing	1
	Plural-s	5
1	Single words	22

However, the acquisition of the underlying processing mechanism does not imply that, at this point, the structure under investigation is produced accurately in every context; it simply signifies the point in time when a learner is in principle capable of producing the structure.

The emergence criterion aims to capture the first productive use of a linguistic structure, serving as an indicator of the acquisition of the relevant processing mechanism. In order to distinguish between a genuinely productive use of a structure and its application as a formulaic sequence (see Section 3.2), a single instance of a structure in a speech sample is not deemed sufficient evidence. For a syntactic structure to count as acquired, a minimum of three instances of this structure with different words should be present in the learner's speech sample (Pienemann et al., 2006; Pienemann & Lenzing, 2015; Lenzing et al., 2019). In morphology, the morpheme under investigation (e.g. the third person –s) has to occur with both lexical variation (the morpheme applied to different words, as in eat–s, sleep–s) and morphological variation (different morphemes applied to one word, as in walk, walk–s, walk–ed) (Pienemann, 1998a, pp. 145–148).

Applying the emergence criterion to the distributional analysis of learner P20, it becomes apparent that there is only one instance of a stage 6 structure in the data sample. The occurrence of a single structure does not constitute sufficient evidence to claim that this structure has been acquired. Regarding the stage 5 structures, the learner produces six instances of Aux 2nd? questions.

A closer examination of the data reveals that these forms occur with sufficient variation, as the learner produces structures such as *What language do you have?*, *What do you eat?*, or *When do you come from the Mars with a (...) spaceship?*. The absence of evidence for the acquisition of the stage 6 structure combined with evidence of the acquisition of a stage 5 structure places the learner at stage 5 of the PT hierarchy.

Much PT-based research relies on learner corpora, with the majority of these studies focusing on spoken data, although written data have also been investigated (e.g. Håkansson & Norrby, 2007). However, in recent years, the scope of the theory has widened to include other aspects of acquisition, such as comprehension. This expansion necessitates different data and approaches to data collection. An example of a tool for collecting comprehension data is the sentence–picture matching task. In sentence–picture matching tasks, learners are presented with three pictures depicting different items or events. They then hear a word or a sentence describing one of these items/events and have to match the prompt with the picture representing the item/event described by the prompt (Kersten et al., 2010; Buyl & Housen, 2015; Lenzing, 2021). This is illustrated in Figure 14 for the passive sentence *The woman is kissed by the man*. Using this method enables us to investigate whether learners comprehend the passive sentence or interpret it in active voice (*The woman kisses the man*).

Other experimental methods to obtain data include reaction time (RT) experiments.[18] Broadly speaking, RT experiments measure the time it takes for a participant to respond to a stimulus in order to shed light on mental processes – in our case on language processing. An example of an RT experiment used in SLA research is the sentence matching experiment (e.g. Bley-Vroman & Masterson, 1989; Gass, 2001; Verhagen, 2011). Its objective is to find out whether learners are

Figure 14 Sentence–picture matching for the passive sentence: *The woman is kissed by the man* (actors: Emilia & Simon Nottbeck; Lenzing, unpubl.).

---

[18]　For an overview of experimental methods in SLA, see, for example, Jiang (2012) and Jegerski and VanPatten (2014).

able to process ungrammaticalities in the stimuli they encounter. In the experiment, the learners are presented with two sentences in an aural or written form with a delay time between them. The sentences are either grammatical or ungrammatical, and the sentence pairs are either identical or not. The learners' task is to judge as quickly as possible whether the sentence pairs are identical or not and to indicate their decision by pressing one of two buttons on a response box. The focus of the analysis is on the matching sentence pairs, as research has shown that native speakers are faster in identifying matching grammatical sentence pairs (as in example 42) than matching ungrammatical sentence pairs (as in example 43) (Lenzing, 2021, p. 132) (Forster, 1979; Freedman & Forster, 1985).

(42) The old woman is followed by the big elephant.
      The old woman is followed by the big elephant.

(43) The old woman is followed Ø the big elephant.
      The old woman is followed Ø the big elephant.

However, the ungrammaticality effects observed in native speakers do not necessarily surface in the data of L2 learners (e.g. Bley-Vroman & Masterson, 1989; Gass, 2001; Verhagen, 2011). Bley-Vroman and Masterson (1989, p. 208) argue that the reaction times in this experiment are used to 'probe the character of the learner's grammar'. The underlying logic behind this hypothesis is that when learners do not show ungrammaticality effects, they have not acquired the structure under investigation (see also Clahsen & Hong, 1995). In this way, sentence-matching experiments are hypothesised to tap into L2 learners' processing operations. Examples (42) and (43) are taken from a study by Lenzing (2021), who investigated the processing of passive structures by native speakers and L2 learners. She hypothesised that only advanced learners who had acquired the necessary procedures to process passive structures would exhibit ungrammaticality effects. In her study both native speakers and advanced learners were indeed faster in identifying matching grammatical sentences than matching ungrammatical sentences. However, learners at lower stages of acquisition did not show the same ungrammaticality effects as the other two groups of participants. The results thus confirmed the hypothesis that these learners had not acquired the necessary procedures required for the processing of passive structures.[19]

Other RT experiments that have been used within the PT framework include self-paced reading or self-paced listening experiments (Buyl, 2015; Spinner & Jung, 2018). In these experiments, the stimuli – usually sentences – are segmented

---

[19] For other studies using sentence matching in the PT framework, see, for example, Pienemann (1998a) and Schmiderer (2023).

into words or phrases. The learners read the words and/or phrases respectively and press a button to proceed to the next segment. The time they spend on reading a particular segment of a sentence is recorded. The underlying rationale is that the time the learners spend on reading a particular segment mirrors their ease or difficulty in processing this segment. In this vein, longer reading times reflect difficulties in processing. The stimuli in self-paced reading experiments within the framework of PT consist of both grammatical and ungrammatical sentences – for instance, sentences with a missing third person –*s* morpheme, as in *the girl eat* versus *the girl eats*. It is assumed that learners who have not acquired the necessary processing prerequisites to detect the ungrammaticality will not show a delay in their reading time. However, once learners are able to process the ungrammaticality their reading time will increase. In this way, the reading times in the self-paced reading experiment shed light on the acquisition of the processing procedures required to be able to process the ungrammaticalities in the stimuli.

4 Implications for SLA Theory

4.1 How PT Approaches the Explanation of SLA

As we pointed out in Sections 1 and 2.1, PT is based on 'explanation by constraint' rather than on causal explanations. In particular, PT focuses on the constraints implied by the architecture of the human language processor, which are operationalised using a formal theory of language. As VanPatten et al. (2020b, p. 9) pointed out in their introductory chapter to *Theories in Second Language Acquisition*, '[…]one of the roles of theories is to explain observed phenomena'. VanPatten et al. (2020b) presented a list of ten observations about SLA that is based on a more extensive list catalogued by Long (1990a). These observations constitute a key subset of 'explananda' of a theory of SLA. In their edited volume VanPatten et al. (2020a) asked every contributor to set out for their specific approach which of these 'explananda' is addressed by their approach and how this is done. In our contribution to that volume (Pienemann & Lenzing, 2020) we addressed six of the ten observations referred to earlier, particularly Observation 4 that states the following: '[…]learners' output … often follows predictable paths with predictable stages in the acquisition of a given structure' (VanPatten et al., 2020b, p. 10). We emphasised that '[e]xplaining this observation is one of the key aims of PT' (Pienemann & Lenzing, 2020, p. 186) and added Observation 5 as a second focal point of our approach: 'second language learning is variable in its outcome' (VanPatten et al., 2020b, p. 10).

These two explananda (or 'mysteries' as we portrayed them in Sections 1 and 2.1) and the aim to elaborate a theory that explains them gave the initial impetus for the development of PT. It turned out that the theory that emerged also has the capacity to offer explanations of several other 'observations' listed in VanPatten et al.'s (2020b, p. 10–12) volume, in particular the following two, that are addressed by PT via specialised hypotheses:

– Observation 8: 'There are limits on the effect of a learner's L1 on L2 acquisition.'
– Observation 9: 'There are limits on the effects of instruction on L2 acquisition.'

In Section 3.3 we summarised the Developmentally Moderated Transfer Hypothesis that addresses the 'limits on the effect of a learner's first language' (Observation 8) within the PT framework. In Section 5.1 we will summarise another specialised hypothesis entailed in PT, known as the Teachability Hypothesis, that addresses 'limits on the effects of instruction on L2 acquisition' (Observation 9).

Following the logic of PT, all of these 'observations' are explained through constraints, not through causes. The main class of constraints utilised in PT is defined by (language) processability as outlined in Sections 2.2–2.5 and throughout this Element. In Section 3.6 we briefly mentioned that PT accounts for the different developmental trajectories found in the acquisition of German as a first and as a second language (see Pienemann, 1998a, 1998b). One issue that arises from this comparison is why L2 learners do not simply restructure their interlanguage in a way that conforms to the more successful trajectory of the L1 learners. As we indicated in Sections 3.4 and 3.6, the explanation offered by Pienemann (1998a, 1998b) is based on generative entrenchment, a mathematical-philosophical approach to developmental and evolutionary constraints set out by Wimsatt (1986), in other words, by another set of constraints: restructuring is computationally too costly. Following the way generative entrenchment is utilised by Pienemann (1998a, 1998b) to explain why L1 learners and L2 learners stay within the confines of their respective developmental trajectories, generative entrenchment acts as a set of constraints that operate within the confines defined by the processability hierarchy. In other words, each subsequent set of constraints further narrows the options resulting from the first set of constraints – like a riverbed enclosed by concrete walls – to continue the imagery from Section 1.

In the supplementary material (www.cambridge.org/Pienemann) on our new approach toward the predictability of L2 dynamics, we briefly mentioned a third set of constraints that operate on SLA. These are the constraints that operate on dynamical systems and that can determine when the developing L2 system reaches a state where one developmental trajectory is taken rather than another.

4.2 How PT Relates to Other Approaches to SLA

Different theories of SLA are not necessarily competing for the same thing. Whether or not theories of SLA are competitors depends on what it is they want to explain. We noted that PT focuses in particular on two 'explanda' (or 'observations' in the terminology of VanPatten et al., 2020b): (1) staged development (Observation 4) and (2) learner variation (Observation 5), and includes hypotheses about L1 transfer (Observation 8) and about teachability (Observation 9).

Some approaches to SLA are not designed as theories and, by implication, to make predictions, but that does not inherently mean that their observations are in conflict with theory-based approaches such as PT. For instance, as Bardovi-Harlig (2020, p. 52) states about her own chosen framework, the concept-oriented approach, in VanPatten et al.'s (2020a) volume *Theories in Second Language Acquisition*,

> …the concept-oriented approach is an analytic framework rather than a theory. It thus lacks the predictive power of a theory. It does, however, contribute to detailed descriptions of L2 acquisition that take meaning as well as form into account.

When it comes to explaining the aforementioned observations about SLA, Bardovi-Harlig prefaces her answer as follows: 'the functionalist approach [of which the "concept-oriented approach" is one sub-class, MP & AL] offers accounts of two of the observations from Chapter 1: predictable stages and the limitations of instruction' (Bardovi-Harlig 2020, p. 53). These accounts are based on an analysis of 'functional load'. The more linguistic markers are related to one meaning function in a sentence, the lower the functional load on each marker. For instance, in the sentence *They travelled to Rome by car*, directionality is implied in *travel*, *to*, and *by car*. Thus the functional load is low on each of these items. Sentences can be understood more easily when the sentence contains multiple markers for the same function. When it comes to form–meaning mappings, learners have been found to initially use the one-to-one principle (Andersen, 1984), producing one clear invariant form for one function (as, e.g., in the exclusive use of –*ed* on verbs for the marking of past events – at the expense of other possible markers such as *was going*).

As this very brief characterisation of the concept-oriented approach shows, it does not – in any obvious way – entail claims that run counter to corresponding claims made by PT. The explanatory device implicit in PT is fully operationalised and based on a set of processing constraints, thus generating testable predictions. In contrast, the concept-oriented approach does not make predictions. Instead, it offers analyses of form–function relationships that can be applied to the sequence in which forms are used to express functions. In other words, PT's explanatory device and the analysis of form–function relationships operate in entirely different ways within the two approaches because those approaches have different objectives. At present, the possible interrelationship between the two approaches is unexplored. It may, however, be quite possible that they will be able to complement each other. Indeed, we agree with VanPatten et al. (2020a, xii) that '[…] we may […] need multiple complementary theories to account for different observed phenomena of SLA[…]'.

There are, nevertheless, specific claims where theories are in competition with each other. One such case relates to different approaches to L1 transfer. As we pointed out in Section 3.3, PT implies a specific hypothesis about the effect of the L1 in L2 acquisition. According to the Developmentally Moderated Transfer Hypothesis (DMTH), L1 transfer is constrained by processability. The DMTH stands in stark contrast to the Full Transfer/Full Access Hypothesis (FT/FA) (Schwartz & Sprouse, 1996) that has been summarised as follows by Schwartz & Sprouse (1996, p. 1):

> FT/FA hypothesizes that the initial state of L2 acquisition is the final state of L1 acquisition (Full Transfer) and that failure to assign a representation to input data will force subsequent restructurings, drawing from options of UG (Full Access).

In this context, the term 'initial state' refers to the learner's implicit knowledge about language at the beginning of the L2 acquisition process, and UG refers to universal grammar, a hypothetical implicit depository of abstract knowledge about principles of languages that all humans have access to. In other words, the FT/FA states that at the start of L2 acquisition learners will transfer the complete structure of the L1 to the L2, and where this strategy fails, they will restructure their assumptions to conform to the L2, drawing on UG.

Unlike the (potentially complementary) relationship between PT and the concept-oriented approach, the DMTH and the FT/FA hypothesis are fundamentally different in two respects: (1) The explanatory mechanisms of the DMTH are derived from constraints on language processing, whereas the FT/FA hypothesis is derived from the assumption that there is a set of abstract principles about possible and impossible structures of language. (2) For specific L1–L2 constellations the two approaches generate contradictory predictions. Both sets of predictions have been tested empirically (see Pienemann, 2011a for an overview). The problem that remains is that each approach has its own view on what constitutes valid data and which methodology must be used to test the predictions. So far, no agreement has been reached on (1) the standards empirical data must meet and (2) how to interpret the available empirical data in a way that satisfies the methodological implications of both approaches.

In the evolution of PT, specifying in detail what must be contained in the initial state has not been a major focus. However, there is potential to work out such a theory component because PT utilises a theory of grammar (LFG) that entails specific views on which forms and principles are shared across languages. There is an additional aspect that would strengthen such an endeavour. Compared to the UG approach advanced by White (2020), the overall architecture of PT – with its sets of constraints on processing, entrenchment and dynamics – requires less information to be contained in the initial state. The UG approach argues that learners display knowledge of linguistic principles that were not contained in the input and that therefore these principles must be innate. In contrast, PT can make use of the logic inherent in generative entrenchment that shows that not all properties that appear in development (such as the exact orientation of the body plan of an organism – as explained in Info Box 3) must be specified in the initial state. Instead, such properties may develop as a result of developmental constraints.

Such a new component of PT that specifies aspects of the initial state would address Observation 3 of the list of explananda discussed by VanPatten et al. (2020b, p. 10): '[l]earners come to know more than what they have been exposed to in the input'. Given the difference between LFG and the grammatical theories utilised by White (2020) and the inclusion of psycholinguistic, entrenchment, and complexity principles in PT, such a new component would take a radically different shape from what is assumed by White (2020), with far less information contained in the initial state and more observations (about SLA) explained by psycholinguistic, entrenchment, and complexity principles.

A third kind of relationship between approaches is apparent overlap. Complex Dynamic Systems Theory (CDST) (see Larsen-Freeman, 2020) and related approaches (e.g. de Bot et al., 2007; see Section 2.1) may appear to overlap with dynamical aspects of PT and even more with our new approach towards the predictability of L2 dynamics (see supplementary material www.cambridge.org/Pienemann), that complements PT and interacts with PT. Both PT and CDST focus on L2 variation. However, as pointed out by Pienemann (2007), CDST views L2 variation as a feature that materialises in variable accuracy scores over time that are attributed to the unsteadiness of the L2 as a dynamical system, whereas PT entails a framework that formally delineates the range within which L2 variation can occur and how it is related to L2 development.

5 Implications for Pedagogy

5.1 The Teachability Hypothesis

This section explores the implications of the existence of developmental sequences in the L2 acquisition of specific morphological and syntactic structures for language teaching. If the developmental sequences observed in numerous empirical studies can be explained by the architecture of the human language processor and the constraints on processability, what does this imply for teaching grammar in the foreign language classroom? Can teaching alter the observed L2 developmental sequences outlined in Section 2.4?

The question of the teachability of a second language began to be addressed systematically in the 1980s in light of the findings that the natural sequence of acquisition observed in L2 learners was also found in instructed settings (see, e.g., Pica, 1983; Ellis, 1989). Pienemann (1984, 1989, 1998a) proposed the Teachability Hypothesis, which makes specific predictions about the scope of the influence that teaching can have on L2 development. The initial version of the teachability hypothesis was based on different theoretical assumptions about the processes underlying developmental sequences in SLA. However, its core claims were later embedded in the theoretical framework of PT. These core claims are:

- stages of acquisition cannot be skipped through formal instruction,
- instruction will be beneficial if it focuses on structures from 'the next stage'

(Pienemann, 1998a, p. 250).

The first claim addresses the question of whether formal teaching can change the developmental sequences found in learner language. Can learners skip stages of acquisition when they are presented with structures from higher stages of acquisition in the language classroom – for instance, can a learner at stage 2 acquire the stage 5 structure third person *–s* if it is taught in the EFL classroom? The Teachability Hypothesis claims that they cannot, as the stage 2 learner has not yet acquired the processing prerequisites required to process the stage 5 structure. As the processing procedures are implicationally related (see Section 2.2), the stage 5 processing procedure can only be acquired once the procedures associated with previous stages are in place.

At first glance, this assumption leads to the impression that the inherent constraints learners face in SLA do not leave room for the formal instruction of grammatical structures. However, the second claim of the Teachability Hypothesis targets potential benefits of teaching. If the structures that are introduced in the language classroom are located at the 'next' developmental stage and learners are thus 'developmentally ready' to acquire these structures, teaching can indeed be beneficial in that it can support learners in advancing to the next stage. This means that while instruction cannot change the route of acquisition, it can have an influence on its rate. In addition, instruction that targets structures that learners are developmentally ready for can influence the frequency of the application of specific features as well as the different contexts in which features are applied (see Section 2.5).

The notion of 'developmental readiness' is crucial to this claim, as it denotes the point in time at which a learner can, in principle, acquire a particular structure. According to Roos (2019, p. 286), developmental readiness 'defines the margin within which instruction may have an effect on the acquisition of specific target language structures [...]'. As we will see, this does not necessarily imply that all learners who are at a particular stage of development will move on to the next developmental stage after having received instruction.

The claims of the Teachability Hypothesis have been investigated in numerous studies (e.g. Pienemann, 1984; Spada & Lightbown, 1999; Mansouri & Duffy, 2005; Di Biase, 2008; Bonilla, 2015; Zhang & Lantolf, 2015; Baten, 2019; see Baten & Keßler, 2019 for a comprehensive overview). The vast majority of the studies support the first claim of the Teachability Hypothesis stating that stages of acquisition cannot be skipped through formal instruction. For instance, the study by Baten (2019) examined the acquisition of the case system by eighteen L2 learners of German. The learners were at stage 2 and stage 3 of acquisition and received instruction on a stage 4 structure. The results showed that none of the learners skipped stages. Thus they all adhered to the prediction of the Teachability Hypothesis.

The study by Zhang and Lantolf (2015) does not support the claims of the Teachability Hypothesis and is thus an exception needing consideration. Zhang and Lantolf investigated the L2 acquisition of a particular Chinese syntactic structure by four learners with English as L1. They argue that the learners in the study were able to skip a stage of acquisition and to progress directly from stage 2 to stage 4 without producing the stage 3 structure targeted in the study. However, the discussions of the study by Baten & Keßler (2019) as well as by Pienemann (2015) cast doubt on this claim, as the stage 3 structure the study focused on is not obligatory in Chinese. This means that the learners involved in the study might have used different structures located at various stages of acquisition to realise their communicative intention.

The second claim of the Teachability Hypothesis engages with potential benefits of instruction for learners who are developmentally ready to acquire structures from the next developmental stage. Here, the study results appear inconclusive. Whereas the claim is clearly supported by a number of studies (e.g. Pienemann,

1984; Di Biase, 2008), other studies yield mixed results (e.g. Spada & Lightbown, 1999; Baten, 2019): some of the learners who were categorised as developmentally ready progressed to the next stage after having been exposed to the respective structures whereas others did not. In addition, some learners at lower stages (stage 2) who were not considered developmentally ready to acquire the structures focused on in the instruction (stage 4) also progressed to the next stage (stage 3). Some researchers (e.g. Spada & Lightbown 1999) have interpreted these findings as counterevidence to the Teachability Hypothesis. However, in all these studies, all learners adhered to the proposed processing constraints, as they did not skip stages. As Baten (2019, p. 319f.) argues,

> two of the misunderstandings concerning the Teachability Hypothesis are (1) that all ready learners will proceed to the next stage and (2) that the unready will not develop at all. This is not what the Teachability Hypothesis … says. On the contrary, the Teachability Hypothesis states that development is constrained and that stages cannot be skipped; it does not state that developmental readiness guarantees acquisition, nor that unreadiness excludes development.

5.2 A Developmentally Moderated Focus on Form in L2 Teaching

The developmentally moderated focus on form approach to L2 teaching (Di Biase, 2002, 2008) builds on the insights of the Teachability Hypothesis and, in particular, on the concept of 'developmental readiness'. As discussed in the preceding section, instruction that focuses on the learner's next stage – that is, instruction that takes the learner's developmental readiness into account – can be beneficial in that it supports the L2 learner's progression to the 'next' developmental stage. Di Biase (2008, p. 1) argues that the learners' developmental readiness should not only guide the selection of linguistic structures introduced in the L2 classroom but also inform the feedback that is provided to the learners regarding their production of the structures that have been selected for them.

Di Biase integrates the notion of developmental readiness with the 'focus on form approach' to language teaching (Long, 1988, 1991, 2015). According to Long (1991, pp. 45–46.), a focus-on-form approach 'overtly draws students' attention to linguistic elements as they arise incidentally in lessons whose overriding focus is on meaning or communication'. This approach stands in contrast to a 'focus on forms' approach, which typically focuses on the explicit teaching of specific linguistic structures and their practice in grammar exercises. Long (1998, p. 37) points out that '[f]ocus on forms lessons tend to be rather dry, consisting principally of work on the linguistic items, which students are expected to master one at a time, often to native speaker levels, with anything less treated as "error," and little if any communicative L2 use'.

In combining the notions of developmental readiness and focus on form, the approach to L2 teaching proposed by Di Biase not only includes a developmentally moderated syllabus that introduces linguistic structures in accordance with the developmental sequences in L2 acquisition but also incorporates feedback targeting structures the learner is developmentally ready for. Di Biase suggests that the overall teaching approach should be meaning-based with the primary emphasis on communicative interaction.

The use of tasks focusing on particular linguistic structures (e.g. Ellis 2003, 2009a) provides opportunities for learners to produce the targeted linguistic forms. The teacher can then provide feedback on the structures the learner is developmentally ready for. This 'developmentally moderated feedback' is directed at any problems that arise with the production or comprehension of the developmentally targeted structures (Di Biase, 2008, p. 4). The feedback concentrates on the learners' spoken production of the linguistic structures under scrutiny and can manifest in various forms, including implicit types like recasts.[20] In this case the teacher reformulates the learner's utterance, correcting the erroneous part, as exemplified in (44):

(44) Learner: Every day the boy go to school.
      Teacher: Every day the boy goes to school.

However, the teacher can also provide more explicit feedback, such as the explicit correction of an error, as illustrated in (45).

(45) Learner: On May.
      Teacher: Not on May, in May. We say, "It will start in May."
      (Ellis, 2009b, p. 9).

The core assumption of the developmentally moderated focus on form approach to L2 teaching is that combining a developmentally moderated syllabus with developmentally sensitive feedback enhances L2 learners' gains in both accuracy and language development. These hypotheses have been supported by empirical studies (e.g. Di Biase 2008; see Info Box 5). The notion of a developmentally moderated approach to language teaching characterised by a focus on developmental readiness and the use of tasks with a focus on form in the language classroom has also been embraced by Keßler and Liebner (2016) as well as by Roos (2019; see Info Box 6).

---

[20] For a comprehensive review of research on the effectiveness of recasts, see Nicholas et al. (2001).

INFO BOX 5 DEVELOPMENTALLY MODERATED FOCUS ON FORM

Bruno Di Biase

What the study is about and why it is important

Developmentally Moderated Focus on Form (DMFonF) is a second language instructional approach that integrates PT's concept of developmental readiness and the Teachability Hypothesis (Pienemann, 1984, 1998a) with Focus on Form (FonF) (Long, 1991).[21] Investigating the potential of DMFonF (Di Biase, 2002, 2008) was necessary because no traditional or current L2 instructional approaches, including meaning-based communicative or task-based approaches, involve developmental moderation.

Research design

The informants were pupils in three Sydney primary schools with a stable Italian L2 programme. These schools had at least two Grade 3 class groups of about fifteen L2 learners each, with the same teacher. This condition enabled one experimental and one control group per school. Initially, the researchers and the teacher identified, through a pre-test, the learners' current L2 developmental stages and accordingly designed a syllabus that gradually presented, through specifically designed tasks, the next stage within the meaning-based lessons.

Following ethical requirements, the control group received the same programme as the experimental group. Fortunately, it was possible to differentiate the feedback in the two groups. So the researcher asked the teacher to provide feedback in the control group on any lexical, grammatical, or pronunciation issues as they saw fit. However, in the experimental group the teacher was asked to ignore any issues arising and to provide feedback exclusively when it concerned the grammatical form that was being taught, thus ensuring that both instruction and feedback were aligned with the learner's development. Once that next stage was well established among learners, the teacher progressed to the following PT stage.

The quasi-experimental research design involves a *Pre-test* (carried out between December and January – that is, between the end of school terms and the beginning of the next school year) followed by the *Treatment* – that is, developmentally scheduled instruction and feedback (between March and early June), and finally a *Delayed Post-test* (six weeks after treatment). Tests were administered face to face with each individual pupil.

---

[21] This investigation was supported by ARC/SPIRT grant C59906982 and CoAsIt NSW as Industry partner.

INFO BOX 5 (cont.)

Through twenty picture description stimuli the individually administered pre-test disclosed that, after more than two years of a two-hours-per-
week meaning-based programme, most pupils acquired at least forty
Italian forms each (nouns, fewer adjectives, greetings). However, with
few exceptions, no form variation was found. Thus, surprisingly, the
children were all at stage 1 (single words and formulae).

An instructional programme was then designed with tasks appropriate for
the next two PT stages: category procedure (marking of plural number on
noun) followed by phrasal procedure (adjectives agree with the noun in the
NP).

Italian marks number (singular or plural) on the noun. The number
marker is different for the two grammatical genders and the three major
noun classes, and it determines the form of the adjective and other
elements within the noun phrase. Tables 13 and 14 show the complexity
of Italian form variation in nouns and adjectives.

Table 13 Italian noun forms (major classes only)

Singular	Plural	Gender* (Eg)
-o	-i**	masculine (letto/letti → bed/beds)
-a	-e	feminine (sedia/sedie → chair/chairs)
-e	-i	masc/fem (pesce (m)/pesci → fish/fishes)
		(mente (f)/ menti →mind/minds)

* Gender and class are inherent to the Italian NOUN lexical entry.
** Given its prevalence and breadth of application the **-i** ending is taken as
default for plural marking in Italian L2.

Table 14 Italian adjective forms (major classes only)

Singular	Plural	Gender (Eg)
-o	-i	masculine (giallo/gialli →yellow)
-a	-e	feminine (gialla/gialle →yellow)
-e	-i	masc/fem (celeste/celesti → sky blue)

(Adjective's gender and number agree with the Noun's)
The Italian adjective has no inherent gender – it will follow the gender of the
NOUN head of phrase – but it has inherent class **(-o/-e)** which constrains the
form the adjective takes in phrasal agreement.

INFO BOX 5 (cont.)

Stage 3 noun–adjective agreement and their unifying features and values are shown in Figure 15, which is a partial LFG representation of the Italian plural noun phrases *libri nuovi* (new books) and *macchine veloci* (fast cars).

Following careful analysis of the number–gender forms, tasks were used focusing on each specific teaching objective – for example, pictures of animals, shapes, or objects requiring the default masculine *-o/-i* alternation in nouns. Once this was established the teacher progressed with tasks focusing on the alternation -a/-e for the largest feminine noun class, and so very gradually moved to other major alternations.

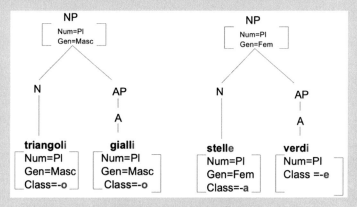

Figure 15 Italian NP plural morphology.

Results

More than two months after the last DMFonF intervention, the delayed post-test, satisfying PT's emergence criteria for morphology (not accuracy), revealed that:

- All children tested in both experimental and control groups reached stage 2 – that is, were able to mark the default *-i* plural in nouns or adjectives.
- All experimental group children and most children (63%) in the control group achieved stage 3 – that is, acquired phrasal marking of plural.
- More experimental group children also marked non-default plural forms than control group children.

INFO BOX 5 (cont.)

Things to consider

- The quasi-experimental project revealed that integrating a DMFonF component in a meaning-based communicative programme is effective in accelerating the pace of acquisition.
- Focused feedback increases accuracy.
- Like other instructed L2 research this experiment confirms that the learners acquisitional path follows PT stages.

INFO BOX 6 TASKS HAVE A GREAT POTENTIAL FOR TARGETED LANGUAGE LEARNING IF THEY INCLUDE A FOCUS ON THE DEVELOPMENTAL READINESS OF L2 LEARNERS

Jana Roos

What the study is about and why it is important

This info box reports on a classroom-based intervention study. The study examined whether using communicative tasks that include a focus on a grammatical feature for which learners are developmentally ready and that engage learners in using that grammatical feature in meaning-focused communication in English lessons can support learners to acquire that feature. The results indicate that providing learners with opportunities to productively use a grammatical feature that is learnable can promote the acquisition of that feature.

Research design

- Twelve German secondary school learners of English were involved in the study. They were selected from two classes in years 6 (six students, ages eleven and twelve) and 7 (six students, ages twelve and thirteen). All of them had been learning English for three and a half years.
- The study focused on the acquisition of 'third person singular -s' (3sg -s, a morphological feature that is introduced early in German textbooks for English as a foreign language but acquired at a relatively late stage in the acquisition process). It is located at stage 5 of the PT hierarchy.
- In order to determine if the learners had acquired 3sg -s, the study followed a pre-test, post-test, delayed post-test design using oral communication tasks that provided multiple contexts for the use of this grammatical feature. In the pre-test eight of the twelve learners had already reached stage 5 in the acquisition of English. The other four

Info Box 6 (cont.)

learners had reached stage 4 and were classified as developmentally ready to acquire 3sg -s. The limited number of occurrences of 3sg -s in their data did not permit conclusions regarding the acquisition of this structure. The pre-test was followed by a two-week instructional period that included an extensive use of communicative tasks designed to provide many contexts for the use of 3sg -s and thus for an implicit focus on form.

- A post-test was carried out immediately after the instructional period and the learners were tested again four weeks later to see if there was a longer-term effect.

Results

- The findings show that from pre-test to post-test the production of 3sg -s increased for all learners. In the case of the four learners who had been shown to be 'ready' to acquire 3sg -s, the use of this grammatical feature increased considerably, which indicates that the classroom intervention led to the acquisition of the targeted structure.
- The data also show a parallel development on the level of syntax: some learners had not produced Aux-2nd-?, another stage 5 structure, in the pre-test, but they did so after the instructional period. This development was probably supported by the tasks that were used in the study, as they required learners to use question forms.
- These findings suggest that second language development in the EFL classroom can be promoted by tailoring instructional intervention to learners' developmental stages through the use of tasks with a 'developmentally moderated focus on form' that engage learners in the active use of the targeted grammatical feature.

Things to consider

It needs to be borne in mind that the number of learners involved in the study was relatively small and the focus was on only one developmental feature. Further studies need to be carried out to show if the use of tasks targeting other grammatical features leads to similar effects.

6 The Constructive Strategy of PT in Theory Building

The construction of Processability Theory is an ongoing process that spans well over twenty-five years at the time of writing these lines. A key strategy underlying this long-term process has been to focus on one 'explanandum' after another, thus developing one compatible theory component after another.

As we have pointed out, PT initially focused on the developmental problem (i.e. why are there stages of development?) and on explaining the range of variation possible between learners. The main explanatory mechanism used in this context was the processability hierarchy in conjunction with feature unification. This device was able to reliably predict morphological and word order development for different Germanic languages (as L2s) (see Pienemann, 1998a).

When this explanatory device was applied to languages that rely less on word order as a marker of grammatical functions such as 'subject', including Arabic, Chinese, and Japanese, it turned out that it generated fewer predictions for L2 development in those languages. In order to account for the development of linguistic features of typologically different languages, Pienemann, Di Biase, and Kawaguchi (2005) constructed an additional L2 developmental hierarchy that is based inter alia on the mapping of arguments (such as 'agent') onto grammatical functions (such as 'subject'). This additional hierarchy turned out to be highly productive in generating developmental predictions for non-Indo-European languages, including Arabic (Mansouri, 2005), Chinese (Zhang, 2005), and Japanese (Kawaguchi, 2005) that have all been substantiated in empirical studies (see Sections 2.6 and 3.5, and Info Box 1 on L2 Japanese).

The limited effect of formal instruction on L2 development had been documented by Pienemann (1984, 1989) before the construction of PT. At the time, it was explained by an isolated set of psycholinguistic hypotheses for German as an L2. With the construction of PT, the predictions for pedagogy were integrated in the cross-linguistic framework provided by PT and could thus be applied cross-linguistically and to a wide range of linguistic phenomena (for details see Section 5.1).

The ability to explain the limited effect of the L1 on L2 acquisition was a natural outgrowth of the theoretical positions informing the construction of PT and many diverse observations of L2 acquisition in typologically different contexts that all had in common a developmental moderation of L1 effects on the developing L2. PT provided a framework that permitted us to formalise and operationalise developmental moderation as a testable hypothesis.

At the very beginning of SLA, learners may exhibit linguistic behaviour that may, at first glance, appear atypical, including whole sentences that may be grammatically correct. Lenzing (2013, 2015) developed an approach to early L2 learner language that deals with such phenomena as formulaic sequences and that complements PT. Lenzing's approach to formulaic utterances includes a formal definition of the term, a methodology for the identification of formulaic sequences, and an account of their communicative functions in the overall context of SLA.

A fundamental issue in the construction of a theory of SLA concerns the relationship between production and comprehension. Recently, Lenzing (2021) added a theory component to PT that deals with this issue at a theoretical and empirical level. Lenzing showed that, in principle, the same processing procedures that are involved in L2 speech production are also used in L2 comprehension. However, as processing resources become available stepwise, initially L2 comprehension needs to take an alternative (semantic) route. All of these concepts and constructs are operationalised and tested using a range of methods specifically developed for this purpose (see Sections 3.1 and 3.7).

The construction of PT continues in the manner outlined earlier in this Element. One of the current projects is the development of an automatic profiling system that can generate an analysis of all developmental and variational features of a learner based on a speech sample collected by the system.

7 Key Readings

Lenzing, A. (2013). *The Development of the Grammatical System in Early Second Language Acquisition: The Multiple Constraints Hypothesis.* Amsterdam: Benjamins. https://doi.org/10.1075/palart.3.

Lenzing, A. (2015). Exploring regularities and dynamic systems in L2 develop ment. *Language Learning*, 65(1), 89–122. https://doi.org/10.1111/lang.12092.

Lenzing, A. (2019). Towards an integrated model of grammatical encoding and decoding in SLA. In A. Lenzing, H. Nicholas, & J. Roos (eds.), *Widening Contexts for Processability Theory: Theories and Issues.* Amsterdam: Benjamins, pp. 13–48. https://doi.org/10.1075/palart.7.02len.

Lenzing, A. (2021). *The Production–Comprehension Interface in Second Language Acquisition: An Integrated Encoding–Decoding Model.* London: Bloomsbury Academic.

Pienemann, M. (1998a). *Language Processing and Second Language Development: Processability Theory.* Amsterdam: Benjamins. https://doi .org/10.1075/sibil.15.

Pienemann, M. (1998b). Developmental dynamics in L1 and L2 acquisition: Processability Theory and generative entrenchment. *Bilingualism: Language and Cognition*, 1, 1–20. https://doi.org/10.1017/S1366728998000017.

Pienemann, M. (ed.) (2005b). *Cross-Linguistic Aspects of Processability Theory*. Amsterdam/Philadelphia: Benjamins. https://doi.org/10.1075/sibil.30.

Pienemann, M., & Keßler, J.-U. (eds.) (2011). *Studying Processability Theory: An Introductory Textbook*. Amsterdam: Benjamins. https://doi.org/10.1075/palart.1.

Pienemann, M., & Lenzing, A. (2020). Processability Theory. In B. VanPatten, G. D. Keating, & S. Wulff (eds.), *Theories in Second Language Acquisition: An Introduction*. 3rd edition. New York: Routledge, pp. 162–191.

References

Andersen, R. W. (1984). The one-to-one principle of interlanguage construction. *Language Learning*, 34, 77–95. https://doi.org/10.1111/j.1467-1770.1984.tb00353.x.

Artoni, D., & Magnani, M. (2013). LFG contribution in second language acquisition research: The development of case in Russian L2. In M. Butt & T. H. King (eds.), *Proceedings of the LFG13 Conference*. Stanford, CA: CSLI, pp. 69–89.

Artoni, D., & Magnani, M. (2015). Acquiring case marking in Russian as a second language: An exploratory study on subject and object. In C. Bettoni & B. Di Biase (eds.), *Grammatical Development in Second Languages: Exploring the Boundaries of Processability Theory*. Paris: Eurosla, pp. 177–193.

Bardovi-Harling, K. (2020). One functional approach to L2 acquisition: The concept-oriented approach. In B. VanPatten, G. D. Keating, & S. Wulff (eds.), *Theories in Second Language Acquisition: An Introduction*. 3rd edition. New York: Routledge, pp. 40–62. https://doi.org/10.4324/9780429503986-3.

Baten, K. (2011). Processability Theory and German case acquisition. *Language Learning*, 61(2), 455–505. https://doi.org/10.1111/j.1467-9922.2010.00615.x.

Baten, K. (2013). *The Acquisition of the German Case System by Foreign Language Learners*. Amsterdam: Benjamins. https://doi.org/10.1075/palart.2.

Baten, K. (2019). Teaching the German case system: A comparison of two approaches. In A. Lenzing, H. Nicholas, & J. Roos (eds.), *Widening Contexts for Processability Theory: Theories and Issues*. Amsterdam: Benjamins, pp. 301–326. https://doi.org/10.1075/palart.7.13bat.

Baten, K., & Keßler, J.-U. (2019). Research timeline. The role of instruction: Teachability and processability. In R. Arntzen, G. Håkansson, A. Hjelde, & J.-U. Keßler (eds.), *Teachability and Learnability across Languages*. Amsterdam: Benjamins, pp. 9–26. https://doi.org/10.1075/palart.6.01bat.

Baten, K. & Ponnet, A. (2023). Extending PT to split ergative marking and differential object marking: Some hypotheses for L2 Hindi. In S. Kawaguchi, Y. Yamaguchi, & B. Di Biase (eds.), *Processability and Language Acquisition in the Asia-Pacific Region*. Amsterdam: Benjamins, pp. 91–114. https://doi.org/10.1075/palart.9.04bat.

Beattie, G., & Shovelton, H. (1999). Do iconic hand gestures really contribute anything to the semantic information conveyed by speech? An experimental investigation. *Semiotica*, 123, 1–30. http://dx.doi.org/10.1515/semi.1999.123.1-2.1.

Bettoni, C., & Di Biase, B. (2015). Processability Theory: Theoretical bases and universal schedules. In C. Bettoni & B. Di Biase (eds.), *Grammatical Development in Second Languages: Exploring the Boundaries of Processability Theory.* Paris: Eurosla, pp. 19–79.

Biber, D., & Reppen, R. (eds.) (2020). *The Cambridge Handbook of English Corpus Linguistics.* Cambridge: Cambridge University Press. https://doi.org/10.1017/S1360674316000277.

Bley-Vroman, R., & Masterson, D. (1989). Reaction time as a supplement to grammaticality judgements in the investigation of second language learners' competence. *University of Hawaii Working Papers in ESL,* 8, 207–245.

Bonilla, C. (2015). From number agreement to the subjunctive: Evidence for Processability Theory in L2 Spanish. *Second Language Research,* 15, 53–74.

Bresnan, J. (ed.) (1982). *The Mental Representation of Grammatical Relations.* Cambridge, MA: MIT Press. https://doi.org/10.2307/414493.

Bresnan, J. (2001). *Lexical-Functional Syntax.* Malden, MA: Blackwell. https://doi.org/10.1002/9781119105664.

Buyl, A. (2019). Is morphosyntactic decoding governed by Processability Theory? In A. Lenzing, H. Nicholas, & J. Roos (eds.), *Widening Contexts for Processability Theory: Theories and Issues.* Amsterdam: Benjamins, pp. 73–101. https://doi.org/10.1075/palart.7.04buy.

Buyl, A., & Housen, A. (2015). Developmental stages in receptive grammar acquisition: A Processability Theory account. *Second Language Research,* 31(4), 523–550. https://doi.org/10.1177/0267658315558590.

Christianson, K., Luke, S. G., & Ferreira, F. (2010). Effects of plausibility on structural priming. *Journal of Experimental Psychology: Learning, Memory, & Cognition,* 36, 538–544. https://doi.org/10.1037/a0018027.

Christianson, K., Williams, C. C., Zacks, R. T., & Ferreira, F. (2006). Younger and older adults' 'good enough' interpretations of garden path sentences. *Discourse Processes,* 42, 205–238. https://doi.org/10.1207/s15326950dp4202_6.

Clahsen, H. (1990). The comparative study of first and second language development. *Studies in Second Language Acquisition,* 12, 135–153. https://doi.org/10.1017/S0272263100009050.

Clahsen, H., & Hong, U. (1995). Agreement and null subjects in German L2 development: New evidence from reaction-time experiments. *Second Language Research,* 11, 57–87. https://doi.org/10.1177/026765839501100103.

Cook, A. E. (2014). Processing anomalous anaphors. *Memory and Cognition,* 42(7), 1171–1185. https://doi.org/10.3758/s13421-014-0415-0.

Dalrymple, M., Dyvik, H., & King, T. H. (2004). Copular complements: Closed or open? In M. Butt & T. H. King (eds.), *Proceedings of the LFG04 Conference.* Stanford, CA: CSLI, pp. 188–198.

Dargue, N., Sweller, N., & Jones, M. P. (2019). When our hands help us understand: A meta-analysis into the effects of gesture on comprehension. *Psychological Bulletin*, 145(8), 765–784. https://doi.org/10.1037/bul0000202.

de Bot, K., Lowie, W. M., & Verspoor, M. H. (2007). A dynamic systems theory approach to second language acquisition. *Bilingualism: Language and Cognition*, 10(1), 7–21. https://doi.org/10.1017/S1366728906002732.

De Houwer, A. (2005). Early bilingual acquisition: Focus on morphosyntax and the separate development hypothesis. In J. F. Kroll & A. M. B. De Groot (eds.), *Handbook of Bilingualism: Psycholinguistic Approaches*. New York: Oxford Academic, pp. 30–48. https://doi.org/10.1093/oso/9780195151770.003.0003.

Di Biase, B. (2002). Focusing strategies in second language development: A classroom-based study of Italian L2 in primary school. In B. Di Biase (ed.), *Developing a Second Language: Acquisition, Processing and Pedagogy of Arabic, Chinese, English, Italian, Japanese, Swedish*. Melbourne: Language Australia, pp. 95–120.

Di Biase, B. (2008). Focus-on-form and development in L2 learning. In J.-U. Keßler (ed.), *Processability Approaches to Second Language Development and Second Language Learning*. Newcastle, UK: Cambridge Scholars, pp. 197–219.

Di Biase, B., Bettoni, C., & Medojević, L. (2015). The development of case: A study of Serbian in contact with Australian English. In C. Bettoni & B. Di Biase (eds.), *Grammatical Development in Second Languages: Exploring the Boundaries of Processability Theory*. Paris: Eurosla, pp. 195–212.

Di Biase, B., & Kawaguchi, S. (2002). Exploring the typological plausibility of Processability Theory: Language development in Italian second language and Japanese second language. *Second Language Research*, 18(3), 272–300. https://doi.org/10.1191/0267658302sr204oa.

Dörnyei. Z., MacIntyre, P., & Henry, A. (eds.) (2015). *Motivational Dynamics in Language Learning*. Bristol, UK: Multilingual Matters. https://doi.org/10.21832/9781783092574.

Dyson, B. P., & G. Håkansson (2017). *Understanding Second Language Processing: A Focus on Processability Theory*. Amsterdam: Benjamins.

Ellis, R. (1989). Are classroom and naturalistic acquisition the same? A study of the classroom acquisition of German word order rules. *Studies in Second Language Acquisition*, 11(3), 303–328. https://doi.org/10.1017/S0272263100008159.

Ellis, R. (2003). *Task-Based Language Learning and Teaching*. Oxford: Oxford University Press.

Ellis, R. (2009a). Task-based language teaching: Sorting out the misunderstandings. *Applied Linguistics*, 19(3), 221–246. https://doi.org/10.1111/j.1473-4192.2009.00231.x.

Ellis, R. (2009b). Corrective feedback and teacher development. *L2 Journal*, 1(1), 3–18. https://doi.org/10.5070/l2.v1i1.9054.

Feldman, D. P. (2019). *Chaos and Dynamical Systems*. Princeton, NJ: Princeton University Press. https://doi.org/10.2307/j.ctvc5pczn.

Ferreira, F. (2003). The misinterpretation of noncanonical sentences. *Cognitive Psychology*, 47, 164–203. https://doi.org/10.1016/S0010-0285(03)00005-7.

Ferreira, F., Bailey, K. G. D., & Ferraro, V. (2002). Good enough representations in language comprehension. *Current Directions in Psychological Science*, 11, 11–15. https://doi.org/10.1111/1467-8721.00158.

Ferreira, F., & Patson, N. D. (2007). The 'good enough' approach to language comprehension. *Language and Linguistics Compass*, 1, 71–83. https://doi.org/10.1111/j.1749-818X.2007.00007.x.

Forster, K. (1979). Levels of processing and the structure of the language processor. In W. E. Cooper & E. Walker (eds.), *Sentence Processing: Psycholinguistic Studies Presented to Merrill Garrett*. Hillsdale, NJ: Lawrence Erlbaum, pp. 27–85.

Freedman, S., & Forster, K. (1985). The psychological status of overgenerated sentences. *Cognition*, 19, 101–131. https://doi.org/10.1016/0010-0277(85)90015-0.

Galileo Galilei (1638). *Discorsi e Dimostrazioni Matematiche Intorno a Due Nuove Scienze: Leida, Appresso gli Elsevirii* (*Mathematical Discourses and Demonstrations, Relating to Two New Sciences*), English translation by Henry Crew and Alfonso de Salvio 1914). https://archive.org/details/bub_gb_E9BhikF658wC/page/n9/mode/2up.

Gambi, C., & Pickering, M. (2017). Models linking production and comprehension. In E. M. Fernández & H. Smith Cairns (eds.), *The Handbook of Psycholinguistics*. Malden, MA: Wiley-Blackwell, pp. 240–268. https://doi.org/10.1002/9781118829516.ch7.

Gass, S. (2001). Sentence matching: A re-examination. *Second Language Research*, 17(4), 421–441.

Håkansson, G., & Norrby, C. (2007). Processability Theory applied to written and oral Swedish. In F. Mansouri (ed.), *Second Language Acquisition Research: Theory-Construction and Testing*. Newcastle, UK: Cambridge Scholars Press, pp. 81–94.

Håkansson, G., Pienemann, M., & Sayehli, S. (2002). Transfer and typological proximity in the context of second language processing. *Second Language Research*, 18(3), 250–273. https://doi.org/10.1191/0267658302sr206oa.

Haldane, J. B. S. (1926). On being the right size. *Harper's Magazine*, 425–427. https://web.archive.org/web/20110822151104/http:/irl.cs.ucla.edu/papers/right-size.html.

Heilbron, J. L. (2010). *Galileo*. Oxford: Oxford University Press.

Hendriks, P. (2014). *Asymmetries between Language Production and Comprehension*. Dordrecht: Springer. https://doi.org/10.1007/978-94-007-6901-4.

Itani-Adams, Y. (2011). Bilingual first language acquisition. In M. Pienemann & J.-U. Keßler (eds.), *Studying Processability Theory: An Introductory Textbook*. Amsterdam: Benjamins, pp. 121–132. https://doi.org/10.1075/palart.1.10bil.

Jegerski, J., & VanPatten, B. (eds.), (2014). *Research Methods in Second Language Psycholinguistics*. New York: Routledge. https://doi.org/10.4324/9780203123430.

Jiang, N. (2012). *Conducting Reaction Time Research in Second Language Acquisition*. New York: Routledge. https://doi.org/10.4324/9780203146255.

Kaplan, R., & Bresnan, J. (1982). Lexical-Functional Grammar: A formal system for grammatical representation. In J. Bresnan (ed.), *The Mental Representation of Grammatical Relations*. Cambridge, MA: MIT Press, pp. 173–281.

Karimi, H., & Ferreira, F. (2016). Good-enough linguistic representations and online cognitive equilibrium in language processing. *Quarterly Journal of Experimental Psychology*, 69(5), 1013–1040. https://doi.org/10.1080/17470218.2015.105395.

Kautzsch, A. (2017). *The Attainment of an English Accent*. Frankfurt: Lang.

Kawaguchi, S. (2005). Argument structure and syntactic development in Japanese as a second language. In M. Pienemann (ed.), *Cross-Linguistic Aspects of Processability Theory*. Amsterdam: Benjamins, pp. 253–298. https://doi.org/10.1075/sibil.30.10kaw.

Kawaguchi, S. (2010). *Learning Japanese as a Second Language: A Processability Perspective*. Amherst, NY: Cambria Press.

Kawaguchi, S. (2015). The development of Japanese as a second language. In C. Bettoni & B. Di Biase (eds.), *Grammatical Development in Second Languages: Exploring the Boundaries of Processability Theory*. Paris: Eurosla, pp. 149–172.

Kawaguchi, S. (2023). Studies of Japanese as a second language and their contribution to Processability Theory. In S. Kawaguchi, B. Di Biase, & Y. Kawaguchi (eds.), *Processability and Language Acquisition in the Asia-Pacific Region*. Amsterdam: Benjamins, pp. 27–62. https://doi.org/10.1075/palart.9.02kaw.

Kempen, G., & Hoenkamp, E. (1987). An Incremental Procedural Grammar for sentence formulation. *Cognitive Science*, 11, 201–258. https://doi.org/10.1016/S0364-0213(87)80006-X.

Kempen, G., Olsthoorn, N., & Sprenger, S. (2012). Grammatical workspace sharing during language production and language comprehension: Evidence from grammatical multitasking. *Language and Cognitive Processes*, 27, 345–380. https://doi.org/10.1080/01690965.2010.544583.

Kersten, K., Rohde, A., Schelletter, C., & Steinlen, A. K. (eds.) (2010). *Bilingual Preschools Volume 1: Learning and Development*. Trier: Wissenschaftlicher Verlag Trier.

Keßler, J.-U., & Liebner, M. (2016). Diagnosing L2-English in the communicative EFL classroom: A task-based approach to individual and developmentally moderated focus on form in a meaning-focused setting. In J. Keßler, A. Lenzing, & M. Liebner (eds.), *Developing, Modelling and Assessing Second Languages*. Amsterdam: Benjamins, pp. 193–205. https://doi.org/10.1075/palart.5.09lie.

Krashen, S., & Scarcella, R. (1978). On routines and patterns in language acquisition and performance. *Language Learning*, 28(2), 283–300. https://doi.org/10.1111/j.1467-1770.1978.tb00135.x.

Lange, M. (2018). Because without cause: Scientific explanations by constraint. In A. Reutlinger & J. Saatsi (eds.), *Explanation beyond Causation: Philosophical Perspectives on Non-causal Explanations*. Oxford: Oxford Academic, pp. 15–38. https://doi.org/10.1093/oso/9780198777946.003.0002.

Larsen-Freeman, D. (2017). Complexity theory: The lessons continue. In L. Ortega & Z. H. Han (eds.), *Complexity Theory and Language Development: In Celebration of Diane Larsen-Freeman*. Amsterdam: Benjamins, pp. 11–50. https://doi.org/10.1075/lllt.48.02lar.

Larsen-Freeman, D. (2020). Complex dynamic systems theory. In B. VanPatten, G. D. Keating, & S. Wulff (eds.), *Theories in Second Language Acquisition: An Introduction*. 3rd edition. New York: Routledge, pp. 248–270.

Lenzing, A. (2013). *The Development of the Grammatical System in Early Second Language Acquisition: The Multiple Constraints Hypothesis*. Amsterdam: Benjamins. https://doi.org/10.1075/palart.3.

Lenzing, A. (2015). Exploring regularities and dynamic systems in L2 development. *Language Learning*, 65(1), 89–122. https://doi.org/10.1111/lang.12092.

Lenzing, A. (2019). Towards an integrated model of grammatical encoding and decoding in SLA. In A. Lenzing, H. Nicholas, & J. Roos (eds.), *Widening Contexts for Processability Theory: Theories and Issues*. Amsterdam: Benjamins, pp. 13–48. https://doi.org/10.1075/palart.7.02len.

Lenzing, A. (2021). *The Production–Comprehension Interface in Second Language Acquisition: An Integrated Encoding–Decoding Model*. London: Bloomsbury Academic.

Lenzing, A. (2022). How a processability perspective frames the potential of tasks in instructed SLA. Keynote, 9th International Conference on Task-Based Language Teaching. University of Innsbruck, 30 August.

Lenzing, A. (forthc./2025). How a processability perspective frames the potential of tasks in instructed SLA. In M. East (ed.), *Broadening the Horizons of TBLT: Plenary Addresses from the Second Decade of the International Conference on Task-Based Language Teaching*. Amsterdam: Benjamins.

Lenzing, A., & Håkansson, G. (2022). Language transfer with regard to grammatical phenomena in L1 German learners of English. In K. Schick & A. Rohde (eds.), *Von integrativem zu inklusivem Englischunterricht*. Frankfurt: Lang, pp. 291–310.

Lenzing, A., Nicholas, H., & Roos, J. (2019). Contextualising issues in processability theory. In A. Lenzing, H. Nicholas, & J. Roos (eds.), Widening Contexts for Processability Theory: Theories and Issues. Amsterdam: Benjamins, pp. 1.8. https://doi.org/10.1075/palart.7.01len.

Lenzing, A., & Pienemann, M. (2015). Response paper: Exploring the interface between morphosyntax and discourse/pragmatics/semantics. In K. Baten, A. Buyl, K. Lochtmann, & M. Van Herreweghe (eds.), *Theoretical and Methodological Developments in Processability Theory*. Amsterdam: Benjamins, pp. 105–112. https://doi.org/10.1075/palart.4.05len.

Lenzing, A., Pienemann, M., & Nicholas, H. (2023). Lost in translation? On some key features of dynamical systems theorizing invoked in SLA research. In K. Kersten & A. Winsler (eds.), *Understanding Variability in Second Language Acquisition, Bilingualism and Cognition*. London: Routledge, pp. 39–79. https://doi.org/10.4324/9781003155683-3.

Levelt, W. J. M. (1981). The speaker's linearization problem. *Philosophical Transactions of the Royal Society of London*, 295(1077, Series B), 305–315. https://doi.org/10.1098/rstb.1981.0142.

Levelt, W. J. M. (1989). *Speaking: From Intention to Articulation*. Cambridge, MA: MIT Press.

Long, M. H. (1988). Instructed interlanguage development. In L. Beebe (ed.), *Issues in Second Language Acquisition: Multiple Perspectives*. Rowley, MA: Newbury House, pp. 115–141.

Long, M. H. (1990a). The least a second language acquisition theory needs to explain. *TESOL Quarterly*, 24, 649–666. https://doi.org/10.2307/3587113.

Long, M. H. (1990b). Maturational constraints on language development. *Studies in Second Language Acquisition*, 12, 251–285. https://doi.org/10.1017/S0272263100009165.

Long, M. H. (1991). Focus on form: A design feature in language teaching methodology. In K. de Bot, R. Ginsberg, & C. Kramsch (eds.), *Foreign*

Language Research in Cross-Cultural Perspective. Amsterdam: Benjamins, pp. 39–52. https://doi.org/10.1075/sibil.2.07lon.

Long, M. H. (2003). Stabilization and fossilization in interlanguage development. In C. Doughty & M. Long (eds.), *The Handbook of Second Language Acquisition Research.* Malden, MA: Blackwell, pp. 487–536. https://doi.org/10.1002/9780470756492.ch16.

Long, M. (1998). Focus on form in task-based language teaching. *Working Papers in ESL University of Hawai'i*, 16(2), 35–49.

Long, M. H. (2015). *Second Language Acquisition and Task-Based Language Teaching.* Malden, MA: Blackwell.

Magnani, M. (2019). Developing morpho-syntax in non-configurational languages: A comparison between Russian L2 and Italian L2. In A. Lenzing, H. Nicholas, & J. Roos (eds.), *Widening Contexts for Processability Theory: Theories and Issues.* Amsterdam: Benjamins, pp. 131–153. https://doi.org/10.1075/palart.7.06mag.

Mansouri, F. (2005). Agreement morphology in Arabic as a second language. Typological features and their processing implications. In M. Pienemann (ed.), *Cross-Linguistic Aspects of Processability Theory.* Amsterdam: Benjamins, pp. 117–153. https://doi.org/10.1075/sibil.30.06man.

Mansouri, F., & Duffy, L. (2005). The pedagogic effectiveness of developmental readiness in ESL grammar instruction. *Australian Review of Applied Linguistics*, 28(1), 81–99. https://doi.org/10.1075/aral.28.1.06man.

Meisel, J. (1989). Early differentiation of languages in bilingual children. In K. Hyltenstam & L. Obler (eds.), *Bilingualism across the Lifespan: Aspects of Acquisition, Maturity and Loss.* Cambridge: Cambridge University Press, pp. 13–40. https://doi.org/10.1017/CBO9780511611780.003.

Meisel, J. (1991). Principles of universal grammar and strategies of language use: On some differences between first and second language acquisition. In L. Eubank (ed.), *Point–Counterpoint: Universal Grammar in a Second Language.* Amsterdam: Benjamins, pp. 231–276. https://doi.org/10.1075/lald.3.12mei.

Meisel, J. (2001). The simultaneous acquisition of two first languages: Early differentiation and subsequent development of grammars. In J. Cenoz & F. Genesee (eds.), *Trends in Bilingual Acquisition.* Amsterdam: Benjamins, pp. 11–41. https://doi.org/10.1075/tilar.1.03mei.

Meisel, J., Clahsen, H., & Pienemann, M. (1981). On determining developmental sequences in natural second language acquisition. *Studies in Second Language Acquisition*, 3(2), 109–135. https://doi.org/10.1017/S0272263100004137.

Mitchell, M. (2009). *Complexity: A Guided Tour.* Oxford: Oxford University Press. https://doi.org/10.1063/1.3326990.

Moser, C., & Smaldino, P. E. (2022). Organizational development as generative entrenchment. *Entropy*, 24(7), 879. https://doi.org/10.3390/e24070879.

Myles, F., & Cordier, C. (2017). Formulaic sequence(fs) cannot be an umbrella term in SLA: Focusing on psycholinguistic FSs and their identification. *Studies in Second Language Acquisition*, 39(1), 3–28. https://doi.org/10.1017/S027226311600036X.

Myles, F., Hooper, J., & Mitchell, R. (1998). Rote or rule? Exploring the role of formulaic language in classroom foreign language learning. *Language Learning*, 48(3), 323–363. https://doi.org/10.1111/0023-8333.00045.

Neuser, H. (2017), *Source Language of Lexical Transfer in Multilingual Learners*. PhD thesis, Stockholm University.

Nicholas, H., Lenzing, A., & Roos, J. (2019). How does PT's view of acquisition relate to the challenge of widening perspectives on SLA? In A. Lenzing, H. Nicholas, & J. Roos (eds.), *Widening Contexts for Processability Theory: Theories and Issues*. Amsterdam: Benjamins, pp. 391–398. https://doi.org/10.1075/palart.7.17nic.

Nicholas, H., Lightbown, P. M., & Spada, N. (2001). Recasts as feedback to language learners. *Language Learning*, 51(4), 719–758. https://doi.org/10.1111/0023-8333.00172.

Nicholas, H., Pienemann, M., & Lenzing, A. (2022a). Predicting stabilisation: The wrong track pathway hypothesis – longitudinal evidence from an adult learner. Paper presented to the PALA Conference, International Islamic University Malaysia, Kuala Lumpur, 21–23 September.

Nicholas, H., Pienemann, M., & Lenzing, A. (2022b). Teacher decision-making, dynamical systems and Processability Theory. *Instructed Second Language Acquisition*, 6, 219–247. https://doi.org/10.1558/isla.21617.

Ortega, L. (2009). *Understanding Second Language Acquisition*. London: Hodder Arnold. https://doi.org/10.4324/9780203777282.

Pica, T. (1983). Adult acquisition of English as a second language under different conditions of exposure. *Language Learning*, 33, 465–497. https://doi.org/10.1111/j.1467-1770.1983.tb00945.x.

Pienemann, M. (1980). The second language acquisition of immigrant children. In S. W. Felix (ed.), *Second Language Development: Trends and Issues*. Tubingen: Narr, pp. 41–56.

Pienemann, M. (1984). Psychological constraints on the teachability of languages. *Studies in Second Language Acquisition*, 6(2), 186–214. https://doi.org/10.1017/S0272263100005015.

Pienemann, M. (1989). Is language teachable? Psycholinguistic experiments and hypotheses. *Applied Linguistics*, 10(1), 52–78. https://doi.org/10.1093/applin/10.1.52.

Pienemann, M. (1998a). *Language Processing and Second Language Development: Processability Theory*. Amsterdam: Benjamins. https://doi.org/ 10.1075/sibil.15.

Pienemann, M. (1998b). Developmental dynamics in L1 and L2 acquisition: Processability Theory and generative entrenchment. *Bilingualism: Language and Cognition*, 1, 1–20. https://doi.org/10.1017/S1366728998000017.

Pienemann, M. (2005a). Discussing PT. In M. Pienemann (ed.), *Cross-Linguistic Aspects of Processability Theory*. Amsterdam: Benjamins, pp. 61–83. https:// doi.org/10.1075/sibil.30.04pie.

Pienemann, M. (ed). (2005b). *Cross-Linguistic Aspects of Processability Theory*. Amsterdam: Benjamins. https://doi.org/10.1075/sibil.30.

Pienemann, M. (2007). Variation and dynamic systems in SLA. *Bilingualism: Language and Cognition*, 10(1), 43–45. https://doi.org/10.1017/S1366728 906002793.

Pienemann, M. (2011a). L1 transfer. In M. Pienemann & J.-U. Keßler (eds.), *Studying Processability Theory: An Introductory Textbook*. Amsterdam: Benjamins, pp. 75–83. https://doi.org/10.1075/palart.1.06lit.

Pienemann, M. (2011b). The psycholinguistic basis of PT. In M. Pienemann & J.-U. Keßler (eds.), *Studying Processability Theory: An Introductory Textbook*. Amsterdam: Benjamins, pp. 27–49. https://doi.org/10.1075/palart.1.03the.

Pienemann, M. (2015). An outline of Processability Theory and its relationship to other approaches to SLA. *Language Learning*, 65, 123–151. https://doi .org/10.1111/lang.12095.

Pienemann, M., Di Biase, B., & Kawaguchi, S. (2005). Extending Processability Theory. In M. Pienemann (ed.), *Cross-Linguistic Aspects of Processability Theory*. Amsterdam: Benjamins, pp. 199–251. https://doi.org/ 10.1075/sibil.30.

Pienemann, M., Di Biase, B., Kawaguchi, S., & Håkansson, G. (2005). Processability, typological distance and L1 transfer. In M. Pienemann (ed.), *Cross-Linguistic aspects of Processability Theory*. Amsterdam: Benjamins, pp. 85–116. https://doi.org/10.1075/sibil.30.05pie.

Pienemann, M. & Keßler, J.-U. (2011) (eds.), *Studying Processability Theory: An Introductory Textbook*. Amsterdam: Benjamins. https://doi.org/10.1075/ palart.1.

Pienemann, M., Keßler, J.-U., & Roos, E. (eds.), (2006). *Englischerwerb in der Grundschule*: *Ein Studien- und Arbeitsbuch*. Paderborn: Schöningh/ UTB.

Pienemann, M., Lanze, F., Nicholas, H., & Lenzing A. (2022). Stabilization: A dynamic account. In A. Benati & J. Schwieter (eds.), *Second Language*

Acquisition as Shaped by the Scholarly Legacy of Michael Long. Amsterdam: Benjamins, pp. 29–76. https://doi.org/10.1075/bpa.14.03pie.

Pienemann, M., & Lenzing, A. (2020). Processability Theory. In B. VanPatten, G. D. Keating, & S. Wulff (eds.), *Theories in Second Language Acquisition. An Introduction*. 3rd edition. New York: Routledge, pp. 162–191.

Pienemann, M., Lenzing, A., & Keßler, J.-U. (2016). Testing the developmentally moderated transfer hypothesis: The initial state and the role of the L2 in L3 acquisition. In J.-U. Keßler, A. Lenzing, & M. Liebner (eds.), *Developing, Modelling and Assessing Second Languages*, Amsterdam: Benjamins, pp. 79–98. https://doi.org/10.1075/palart.5.04pie

Pienemann, M., Lenzing, A., & Nicholas, H. (online first/2024). Can dynamical systems theory be applied to second language acquisition? The issues of reductionism and intentionality. *Second Language Research*. https://doi.org/ 10.1177/02676583241229280.

Pienemann, M., & Mackey, A. (1993). An empirical study of children's ESL development and Rapid Profile. In P. McKay (ed.), *ESL Development: Language and Literacy in Schools*. Volume 2. Melbourne: Commonwealth of Australia and National Languages and Literacy Institute of Australia, pp. 115–259.

Plag, I. (2011). Pidgins and Creoles. In M. Pienemann & J.-U. Keßler (eds.), *Studying Processability Theory: An Introductory Textbook*. Amsterdam: Benjamins, pp. 106–120. https://doi.org/10.1075/palart.1.09pid.

Platzack, C. (1996). The initial hypothesis of syntax: A minimalist perspective on language acquisition and attrition. In H. Clahsen (ed.), *Generative Perspectives on Language Acquisition*. Amsterdam: Benjamins, pp. 369–414. https://doi.org/ 10.1075/lald.14.15pla.

Poesio, M., Sturt, P., Artstein, R., & Filik, R. (2006). Underspecification and anaphora: Theoretical issues and preliminary evidence. *Discourse Processes*, 42, 157–175. https://doi.org/10.1207/s15326950dp4202_4.

Ponnet, A. (2023). *Climbing the Language Tree: Multiple Case Studies on the Acquisition of Hindi as a Foreign Language*. PhD thesis, Ghent University.

Roos, J. (2007). *Spracherwerb und Sprachproduktion: Lernziele und Lernergebnisse im Englischunterricht der Grundschule*. Tubingen: Narr.

Roos, J. (2019). Exploiting the potential of tasks for targeted language learning in the EFL classroom. In A. Lenzing, H. Nicholas, & J. Roos (eds.), *Widening Contexts for Processability Theory: Theories and Issues*. Amsterdam: Benjamins, pp. 285–300. https://doi.org/10.1075/palart.7.12roo.

Schmiderer, K. (2023). *Produktiver und rezeptiver Grammatikerwerb im schulischen Italienischunterricht*. Tubingen: Narr.

Schwartz, B., & Sprouse, R. (1994). Word order and nominative case in nonnative language acquisition: A longitudinal study of (L1 Turkish) German interlanguage. In T. Hoekstra & B. Schwartz (eds.), *Language Acquisition Studies in Generative Grammar: Papers in Honor of Kenneth Wexler from the 1991 GLOW Workshops*. Amsterdam: Benjamins, pp. 317–368. https://doi .org/10.1075/lald.8.14sch.

Schwartz, B., & Sprouse, R. (1996). L2 cognitive states and the full transfer/full access model. *Second Language Research*, 12(1), 40–72. https://doi.org/ 10.1177/026765839601200103.

Segaert, K., Menenti, L., Weber, K., Petersson, K., & Hagoort, P. (2012). Shared syntax in language production and language comprehension: An fMRI study. *Cerebral Cortex*, 22, 1662–1670. https://doi.org/10.1093/cercor/bhr249.

Siegel, J. (2010). Pidgins and Creoles. In R. B. Kaplan (ed.), *The Oxford Handbook of Applied Linguistics*. 2nd edition. Oxford: Oxford Academics. https://doi.org/10.1093/oxfordhb/9780195384253.013.0026.

Simon, H. A. (1962). The architecture of complexity. *Proceedings of the American Philosophical Society*, 106(6), 467–482.

Spada, N., & Lightbown, P. (1999). Instruction, first language influence, and developmental readiness in second language acquisition. *Modern Language Journal*, 83(1), 1–22. https://doi.org/10.1111/0026-7902.00002.

Spinner, P., & Jung, S. (2018). Production and comprehension in Processability Theory: A self-paced reading study. *Studies in Second Language Acquisition*, 1–24. https://doi.org/10.1017/S0272263117000110.

Turnbull, M. G. (2018). Underdetermination in science: What it is and why we should care. *Philosophy Compass*, 13(2), https://doi.org/10.1111/ phc3.12475.

VanPatten, B. (2020). Input processing in adult L2 acquisition. In B. VanPatten, G. D. Keating, & S. Wulff (eds.), *Theories in Second Language Acquisition: An Introduction*. 3rd edition. New York: Routledge, pp. 105–127.

VanPatten, B., Keating, G. D., & Wulff, S. (eds.) (2020a). *Theories in Second Language Acquisition: An Introduction*. 3rd edition. New York: Routledge. https://doi.org/10.4324/9780429503986.

VanPatten, B., Williams, J., Keating, G. D, & Wulff, S. (2020b). Introduction. The nature of theories. In B. VanPatten., G. D. Keating, & S. Wulff (eds.), *Theories in Second Language Acquisition: An Introduction*. 3rd edition. New York: Routledge, pp. 1–18.

Verhagen, J. (2011). Verb placement in second language acquisition: Experimental evidence for the different behaviour of auxiliary and lexical verbs. *Applied Psycholinguistics*, 32, 821–858. https://doi.org/10.1017/ S0142716411000087.

Wheeldon, L. R., & Konopka A. (2023). *Grammatical Encoding for Speech Production*. Cambridge: Cambridge University Press.

White, L. (2020). Linguistic theory, universal grammar, and second language acquisition. In B. VanPatten, G. D. Keating, & S. Wulff (eds.), *Theories in Second Language Acquisition: An Introduction*. 3rd edition. New York: Routledge, pp. 19–39.

Wimsatt, W. C. (1986). Developmental constraints, generative entrenchment, and the innate-acquired distinction. In W. Bechtel (ed.), *Integrating Scientific Disciplines: Science and Philosophy*. Volume 2. Springer: Dordrecht, pp. 85–208. https://doi.org/10.1007/978-94-010-9435-1_11.

Wolpert, L. (1992). The shape of things to come. *New Scientist*, 134(18), 38–42. https://archive.org/details/sim_new-scientist_1992_134_index/page/n1/mode/2up.

Wray, A. (2008). *Formulaic Language: Pushing the Boundaries*. Oxford: Oxford University Press.

Zhang, X., & Lantolf, J. (2015). Natural or artificial: Is the route to L2 development teachable? *Language Learning*, 65, 152–190. https://doi.org/10.1111/lang.12094.

Zhang, Y. (2005). Processing and formal instruction in the L2 acquisition of five Chinese grammatical morphemes. In M. Pienemann (ed.), *Cross-Linguistic Aspects of Processability Theory*. Amsterdam: Benjamins, pp. 155–177. https://doi.org/10.1075/sibil.30.07zha.

Acknowledgements

We would like to thank Howard Nicholas for his thoughtful comments on many aspects of this manuscript, one reviewer for his valuable feedback, Adam Hooper from CUP for his support in getting the many pieces of this Element together, the series editors John W. Schwieter and Alessandro Benati for their encouragement and support, and Katharina Hohengartner and Philomena Kremser for their editorial support. We would also like to thank the authors of the Info Boxes, Bruno Di Biase, Satomi Kawaguchi, Marco Magnani, Howard Nicholas and Jana Roos for their wonderful cooperation.

Cambridge Elements ☰

Second Language Acquisition

Alessandro G. Benati

University College Dublin

Alessandro G. Benati is Professor and Head of the School of Education at University College Dublin. He is visiting and honorary professor at the University of York St. John, Anaheim and the University of Hong Kong. Alessandro is known for his work in second language acquisition and second language teaching. He has published ground-breaking research on the pedagogical framework called Processing Instruction.

John W. Schwieter

Wilfrid Laurier University, Ontario

John W. Schwieter is Associate Professor of Spanish and Linguistics, and Faculty of Arts Teaching Scholar, at Wilfrid Laurier University. His research interests include psycholinguistic and neurolinguistic approaches to multilingualism and language acquisition; second language teaching and learning; translation and cognition; and language, culture, and society.

About the Series

Second Language Acquisition showcases a high-quality set of updatable, concise works that address how learners come to internalize the linguistic system of another language and how they make use of that linguistic system. Contributions reflect the interdisciplinary nature of the field, drawing on theories, hypotheses, and frameworks from education, linguistics, psychology, and neurology, among other disciplines. Each Element in this series addresses several important questions: What are the key concepts?; What are the main branches of research?; What are the implications for SLA?; What are the implications for pedagogy?; What are the new avenues for research?; and What are the key readings?

Cambridge Elements ☰

Second Language Acquisition

Elements in the Series

Proficiency Predictors in Sequential Bilinguals: The Proficiency Puzzle
Lynette Austin, Arturo E. Hernandez and John W. Schwieter

Implicit Language Aptitude
Gisela Granena

Generative Second Language Acquisition
Roumyana Slabakova, Tania Leal, Amber Dudley and Micah Stack

The Acquisition of Aspect in a Second Language
Stefano Rastelli

Focus on Form
Alessandro Benati

Interaction
Jennifer Behney and Susan Gass

Explicit and Implicit Learning in Second Language Acquisition
Bill VanPatten and Megan Smith

Thinking and Speaking in a Second Language
Yi Wang and Li Wei

Pragmatics, Grammar and Meaning in SLA
Aoife K. Ahern, José Amenós-Pons and Pedro Guijarro-Fuentes

Input
John Truscott

Processability Theory
Manfred Pienemann and Anke Lenzing

A full series listing is available at: www.cambridge.org/ESLA

Printed in the United States
by Baker & Taylor Publisher Services